Sculptured
Needlepoint
Stitchery

SCULPTURED
Needlepoint
Stitchery

ELLA PROJANSKY

Charles Scribner's Sons   New York

All photography (except Plate 1 from *McCall's Needlework & Crafts Magazine*) by Doug Long, a New York craft and art photographer.

Library of Congress Cataloging in Publication Data

Projansky, Ella J.
    Sculptured needlepoint stitchery.

    Includes index.
    1. Canvas embroidery—Patterns.   I. Title.
    TT778.C3P76   746.4′4   77-15969
              ISBN 0-684-15371-8

1 3 5 7 9 11 13 15 17 19 MD/C 20 18 16 14 12 10 8 6 4 2

Printed in the United States of America

Acknowledgments

I'm eternally grateful to Lore O'Leary, my highly overqualified assistant; but for her tirelessly devoted efforts in my behalf, this book might never have been completed. My earliest attempts to render the graphs made abundantly clear to both of us that I really can't draw a straight line, even with a ruler. But Lore sure can—and did! All of them. (I only got to do the curved lines.)

When first we met, Lore thought I was a nitpicking fusspot; now that she's become a first-class needlepointer of considerable skill and a nonpareil blocker, she, too, is convinced that "only the best is good enough." Her work truly enhances this volume.

My thanks, too, to Almy Bierregaard and Dorothy Perkins, who, when they gave me my first and only lesson, together planted the seed for this book; to all my students who urged me to write it, I offer my humble appreciation of their confidence in me; and to Elinor Parker and Janet Hornberger of Scribners, I can only express congratulations on their expertise and thanks for their patience and help.

A very special thank you goes to my built-in cheering section: my husband, David; my sons, Robert, Arnold, and Michael; and ten grandchildren, who announced early on that "Gran'ma was gonna get famous" and who never wavered in their faith. I must admit that toward the end of the gestation period I began to dread the more articulate ones who kept asking, "Is it soup yet?"

Well, it seems it's been simmering forever, but here it is, kids. At last, soup's on!

Foreword

In these pages I've attempted to demonstrate that there are many, many ways to design sculptured needlepoint stitchery, as many ways as there are enthusiasts to explore its potentials. My hope, of course, is that you will be one of them. The field is wide open and only your own hesitation can limit you. Don't be put off by the possibility of error; you can learn as much by ripping out as by putting in your stitches. You may even invent a new stitch in the process; I did—several times.

I should, however, caution you that it's not wise to be *so* eager that you plunge in without learning enough for a sound foundation on which to build your creative efforts. There's nothing more frustrating than seeing your nearly finished piece headed for disaster because of some little thing you did or didn't do at the beginning. That's a long way back to go to set things straight, and it's especially irksome to have to acknowledge, if only to yourself, that it could all have been avoided if you'd taken a little time to lay the proper groundwork.

Contents

Sculptured
Needlepoint
Stitchery

Introduction

Sculptured needlepoint stitchery is embroidery on canvas carried into the third dimension, beyond the limits of conventional needlepoint stitches. The design concept utilizes the variable third dimension—depth—of needlepoint stitches in such a way that neither color nor conventional pictorial design is essential to its creation.

Of course, this doesn't mean you can't augment or enhance a conventional needlepoint design. It only means you don't *need* a conventional design to create a sculptured needlepoint stitchery design.

This marvelous new medium comes to life entirely on its own, aided by the fascinating play of light and shadow on the different planes of stitchery. It has been (and still is!) such an exciting challenge that I'm bursting to share it with you.

As you'll soon see, it's a lot simpler than it sounds. Like most things, it's simple to do when you know how. And in practically no time, assuming you want to, you'll know how, too. I promise—and I never promise what I can't deliver.

If you've never done any needlepoint, you're in luck; you have no bad habits to unlearn. Everything you need to know is right here, so relax and read on.

If you are a needlepointer, whether a beginner or a veteran, I'm sure some of what follows will be old hat. But I suggest you go through it all anyway, word for word, because you never know when you'll turn up something new and useful to you.

From my own reading and years of teaching experience, I know I have a lot to tell you about needlepoint and stitchery that you won't find elsewhere and that you'll be glad to know about. For instance, you'll finally discover the truth about the mesh; is it a hole, a square, or something else altogether?

The history of needlepoint is centuries old; the history of needlepoint stitchery is old but somewhat younger. The history of sculptured needlepoint stitchery in this country is very recent. Two of the earliest recorded designs were inspired by the bold drama of the Aran fisherman's knitted sweaters; I designed them for *McCall's Needlework & Crafts Magazine* several years ago. Later I did a couple of small pillows for them in a somewhat simplified

1

version of Irish crochet lace. A mirror frame that followed in sculptured needlepoint stitchery struck a slightly more formal note (Plate 1).

These pioneer efforts are, to my knowledge at least, the only examples of sculptured needlepoint stitchery published to date, which makes this a very young history indeed.

When the earliest of these designs came into existence, I wasn't remotely considering anything like a book. Each piece as it developed was only an experiment in sculptured stitchery for my own edification; I kept few or no records. What few notations I did make were constantly having to be changed or abandoned as I changed and abandoned stitches, trying them, ripping them, trying another, ripping, shifting, ripping, ripping, ripping.

The selection of these particular designs is meant to give you a foretaste of the wide range of design styles that can be developed from sculptured needlepoint stitchery, and to demonstrate how truly versatile ordinary needlepoint stitches can be. And it's only a beginning, as you'll see.

The designs in this book are a mixture of naïveté and sophistication, simplicity and complexity. There is no orderly progression from "easy" to "intermediate" to "advanced" in this collection, as there is in many needlepoint books. I've made no effort to "grade" the simplicity or complexity of any of these designs. I leave all selection and decision making to you. What may, in my judgment as designer and teacher, seem somewhat laborious for a first attempt, may well be a snap for you. Who knows why? Perhaps because the stitch plan or graph appeals to your own body rhythm, or because a couple of stitches are old, familiar favorites. Perhaps a sense of adventure— or maybe you just love the project and can't wait to do it. As we all know, nothing's too difficult if we really want to do it.

The truth of the matter is that generally these designs were meant to be impressive to the beholder but easy enough so that a beginner could be taught by written instruction alone.

I suggest you do a couple of practice pieces so you can get the feel of what sculptured needlepoint stitchery is all about. You may want to make a piece or two to increase your familiarity with some stitches that are new to you. Sculptured needlepoint is a little different from ordinary needlepoint and a little practice can build up a lot of self-confidence, to say nothing of expertise. This may also be a good time to do some sample stitches for your notebook (see Contents).

Examine all the photos, graphs, and stitch guides. Having explored all my designs and illustrations, please read all my preliminary instructions (pages 3–24) thoroughly and carefully. There's some very important, even essential, meat among those dry bones of information, and I'd like to think you didn't miss any of it.

I suppose it's only fair to warn you at the outset that this book reflects one needleworker's biases, and you're free to disregard them (at your own risk, naturally). As my clients and students will attest, my standards in materials, efforts, and results are tough and consistent. Only the best is good enough for me!

Having made noises like a villain, let me hasten to reassure you. I'm really a pussycat and a firm believer that only you can be the judge of what's right for you. Let's agree, then, that I'll go on making very positive statements based on *my* experience and conclusions, and you'll do exactly as you please. O.K.? And so I wish you Happy Stitchery.

What's in It for You?

For each of the designs set forth in this book, you'll have a *color plate* or black-and-white photo of the finished project; a series of *stitch guides* for all the stitches in that particular design, showing you how each stitch is constructed and how to do it; a *graph* to show you where on the canvas the stitches are to be made and how many to make; a *symbol chart* showing the symbols used on the graph to represent the stitches, their names, and the number of plies used in each stitch; plus a black-and-white detail *photo* to show you how the stitches look together on canvas.

I've also given you, as thoroughly as space permits, whatever I know that may be helpful and constructive. Even an old hand at needlepoint can probably still use a little guidance in a new endeavor, since there are always unsuspected pitfalls and obstacles that have to be dealt with. Therefore you'll find in each project section a running commentary, at times explicit, sometimes general, usually pertinent, often informative, and always, I hope, instructive.

The graph, unless otherwise designated, will show one-fourth of the entire design and will represent the upper right-hand quarter of the canvas. The background lines of the graph, both vertical ↕ and horizontal ⟷, are equal to and represent the threads of your canvas; each crossed place is a mesh. On the graph, stitches will be shown by heavy lines as symbols of the real stitches to be placed on the canvas. When the design employs more than one color, or several shades of a color, the stitches will be shown on the graphs by the same system, but there will also be a color guide, by stitch symbol and name: for example, Scotch stitch ⟋⟋⟋ , dark pink. You'll start to stitch from the center of the canvas, which will be shown on the graph by a large arrowhead. Once you've identified the center of your canvas and matched it up with that central arrowhead on your graph, you're ready to go . . . almost.

I agree that it's not necessary to learn all the stitches in this book to do sculptured needlepoint stitchery, but it certainly can't hurt. In a few of my designs you'll find you need to know only three or four stitches. These projects might make good starters if you're nervous about tackling more stitches, although it hardly makes much difference if the eight or nine stitches in another piece are easy to learn and do. Stretch yourself a little; you're capable of reaching heights you've never dreamed of.

The stitch guides are the visible results of my own dissatisfaction with stitch instructions in most books and kits. Far too often, they're inadequate and/or confusing, particularly for the beginner. My own teaching experience and the customer feedback we get from the stitch guides in our kits* have strongly borne out my conviction that it's worth the additional time, effort, and expense to draw each stitch as though it were made of yarn-on-canvas instead of pen-on-paper. The reader should be able to see clearly how each stroke is made, how the stitch begins and proceeds and ends, where the needle goes into the canvas, where it comes out, and where the yarn is while all this is going on.

Someone who has never held a needle before should be able to follow my stitch guides with very gratifying results and be encouraged to go on with sculptured needlepoint stitchery. Too many hopefuls have turned away from stitchery and needlepoint itself because of poor stitch instructions, and that's a pity. They've been denied a whole wide world of pleasure and perhaps even fulfillment because someone was too lazy, ignorant, or pennypinching to provide fully adequate instructions.

My own first contact with needlepoint instructions turned me off completely for nearly thirty-five years! Fortunately, one day I was intrigued by the work of a stranger and was seduced into trying once more. One personal lesson, my first and last, and I was off and running, delirious with the excitement of learning what there was to learn beyond that rudimentary lesson.

Today, ten years and a century of experience later, I'm still somewhat delirious with the excitement of learning my craft. (I've only scratched the surface in the field of Aran knits as design inspiration, and I'm *still* having trouble with cables!)

For your convenience, each design section has all of the stitch guides it needs, no matter how many times they have to be repeated.† You'll be a lot happier not having to juggle graphs, instructions, canvas, needle, yarn, and so on, while you hunt for a particular stitch guide.

I believe easy does it, every time!

---

* Ella Projansky's Needleworks, Inc.

† The two exceptions are the continental stitch and the basketweave stitch, which are so basic and essential that separate sections have been devoted to them (see Contents). These two stitches should, as quickly as possible, become second nature to you; they are the veritable foundation of your entire needlepoint experience.

Canvas
and Yarn

Unlike crewel or embroidery, which simply decorates an attractive cloth background, needlepoint has a totally different objective. Our goal in conventional needlepoint is to cover every bit of the material we're working on. Usually this material is canvas, and ideally it is made of 100 percent long-fiber cotton or linen threads, uniformly round and polished and woven into a fabric resembling window screening. The fabric is stiffened into a kind of grid by a starch solution called sizing, and it comes in three forms: single-thread or monofilament (mono), double-thread (Penelope), and locked-weave (leno).

Of these three, we'll be concerning ourselves only with the first two, *mono* and *Penelope*, which are available in white or ecru in widths of from 18 inches to 72 inches, depending on the gauge. Locked-weave canvas is of no use to us because its rigid, locked mesh will not permit us to manipulate the meshes as we need to for many of our stitches.

This is a blessing in disguise, because locked-weave canvas is always an inferior grade of canvas, generally made of weak, coarse, and short-fibered threads; it depends on its heavy sizing to give the buyer the impression of substance. It was designed by a particular part of the canvas industry to satisfy the needs of mass-market kit makers who were interested in a material that would respond like paper to a heat transfer of design. Try to forget that it exists.

Keeping in mind that needlepoint will last only as long as the canvas it covers, it's generally a good idea when buying canvas to hold it up to the light and examine the holes. Poor-grade canvas will have holes that are clogged with sizing, and a very obvious network of sizing-stiffened fibers chokes the space where your yarn must go. Look for a superior-grade canvas which, when held up to light, will reveal tightly twisted, round, polished threads with few or no fibers showing, so there will be minimal yarn abrasion when you stitch over the meshes.

Which brings us directly to the storm center of the longtime confusion about meshes and what they really are!

Many authors, teachers, designers, and other authorities in the needlepoint world refer to or count the *holes* in needlepoint canvas and call them "mesh" or "meshes." This error stems from a misconception that has long needed to be clarified and corrected. There are two distinctly different types of material constructed or woven of crossed filaments. One type is designed to keep things in or out by the use of holes smaller than the object to be controlled, for example: fishnet, fly screening, wire strainers, chicken-wire fencing, filters, and so on. It is in this type of material that the holes are measured by size gauge ($\frac{1}{16}$ inch, $1\frac{1}{2}$ inches, and so on) and are correctly called "mesh" or "meshes." This does not apply to needlepoint canvas.

The other type of crossed-filament material is any fabric that is designed to have a particular texture created by the number of crossed filaments or threads that form it. The fabrics may be as dissimilar as chiffon, burlap, velvet, and canvas. In the instance of canvas, the needlepoint texture requires that we cover with needlepoint stitches all those places where the canvas threads cross each other. Those crossed-canvas-thread places, measured by number-to-the-inch gauge, are correctly called "mesh" or "meshes."

For us needlepointers, therefore, a mesh is only that place where a horizontal canvas thread and a vertical canvas thread cross each other (see drawings, left).

The most generally satisfactory canvas for sculptured needlepoint stitchery seems to be white mono for use with Persian yarn and white Penelope for shag or rug yarn. Since the ideal sculptured stitchery is executed in medium to light shades (when done in color), there doesn't appear to be any need for that depressing ecru canvas as a foundation, I'm happy to report.

White mono needlepoint canvas of superior grade is available in gauges from #42 (42 pt.) to #10 (10 pt.). Anything coarser or more open-weave than 10 pt. is available only in Penelope (double-thread) canvas, from #9 to #3½ gauge in both white and ecru.

As for what gauges do for us, you're probably already familiar with the difference between a no-nonsense 140-count muslin sheet and a silky-smooth 180-count percale or a luxurious 220-count Supercale bed sheet. These count (gauge) numbers tell you that in a square inch (1 inch $\times$ 1 inch) of sheet fabric you may have either 140, 180, or 220 crossed threads. Obviously, if 220 threads are to be packed into the same area taken up by 140 muslin threads, they're going to have to be much finer and silkier. Similarly, in order to achieve the particular texture we're planning to create on our framework of meshes, we need some kind of guide to tell us how dense or sparse our needlepoint can be.

In needlepoint canvas the gauge number designates the number of mesh to the inch, measured vertically (lengthwise); #10 or 10 pt. means that there are 10 mesh to the running inch and 100 to the square inch. (10 pt., by the way, is a French abbreviation for 10 *points,* or 10 stitches, which bears out the needlepoint "mesh" distinction.)

You'll find good canvas generally available in those needlework shops that consistently carry the very best-quality designs and supplies.

All the designs in this book were done on either French 100 percent long-staple cotton canvas (when available) or on German Zweigart, Superior Grade. At the present writing, there is no French mono canvas available because of the destruction, by fire, of the remarkable old hand-hewn wooden looms. How they'll be replaced is still in question, and you'll have to discover some remaindered stock in order to experience the ultimate in mono needlepoint canvas. Ask at your favorite needlework shop; they may be

HORIZONTAL MESH

VERTICAL MESH

hoarding some. Some French Penelope canvas is still available, however, and I suggest you try to find some for use with shag or rug yarn in #8, #7 or #5.

If you can't find any French canvas, don't despair. You can use Zweigart, Superior Grade, German canvas in both mono and Penelope to achieve excellent results. Be prepared for one slight difference, however. The German gauge (surely male-oriented from that fishnet perspective) counts *holes,* so that 12 gauge in German canvas means 12 holes or *13 threads* to the inch, making the canvas grid slightly more dense, and, if you're counting by mesh or threads as you usually are in sculptured needlepoint stitchery, your finished piece will be slightly smaller than if it were done on the same gauge French canvas. I can't give you an accurate allowance guide, but I'd estimate perhaps an inch difference in 12 to 15 inches on #12. That is, on #12 German mono canvas, 144 stitches would be closer to 11 inches than to 12 inches deep. The character of the stitches you use will also affect size and dimensions, and you'll have to experiment (see "Notebook," page 125).

In any case, buy your canvas by the half-yard, or better yet, if the budget will allow, by the yard; don't be seduced into buying ready-cut pieces, even if they're bound. The canvas you buy off the roll is more likely to be fresh and supple. For real economy, do your own cutting and taping.

The yarn I've used in all my designs, whether 3-ply Persian, 4-ply rug, or 4-ply shag, is all Paternayan yarn—available in 342 glowing colors—long-staple 100 percent virgin wool, adaptable, long-wearing, lustrous, incredibly strong, mothproof, colorfast, washable, dry cleanable, a veritable ideal of wool yarns. I use no other. (I did warn you about bias!)

Paternayan Persian yarn is available in several forms and will probably meet all your requirements. The bulk Persian is available in continuous-thread quarter-pound loops and also in cut strands (approximately 30 to 32 inches long) which are sold in strands or by the ounce (generally 40 strands to the ounce). It is also available in 40-yard skeins and in 8-yard ones. Naturally, it's wise, whenever possible, to buy all the yarn you require for a project at the same time and from the same dye lot, just as you do with knitting yarns.

Incidentally, Paternayan will even dye a special color for you if you need it. The only stipulation is that you order a minimum of 5 pounds of the special color; that's an exclusive service no one else provides.

The canvases I've recommended and Paternayan yarn are sold by every needlework shop that deserves to call itself a quality shop, and you'll probably have no trouble finding one or more in your area.

If you can't find a good source, write to Paternayan Brothers, Inc., 312 East 95th Street, New York, New York 10028. They won't sell to you directly unless you're a bona fide retailer, but they will tell you who sells Zweigart canvas and Paternayan yarn in your area.

I hope you won't attempt to use knitting yarns, which are totally unsuitable. Even the best are twisted of short-fibered yarns, which will not withstand repeated contact with strong canvas threads. To attempt to use them in separated plies guarantees disaster.

In response to the frequent outcry that "the best is too expensive," I'd like to offer a simple exercise in arithmetic.

Let's assume you're contemplating making a needlepoint piece approximately 14 inches × 14 inches. Allowing a 2-inch margin all around for blocking, finishing, and mounting, you will need a square of canvas 18 inches $\times$ 18 inches (2 inches + 14 inches + 2 inches = 18 inches).

You can cut four pieces that size from a yard of needlepoint canvas 36 to 39 inches wide. If you buy cheap canvas at today's inflated prices, your canvas will cost you about $8 a yard and your pillow-size piece (18 inches $\times$ 18 inches) will cost you only $2. Terrific price? You bet!

If you buy the best, it will probably cost you about $15 per yard, which means your pillow-size piece costs $3.50. Your canvas saving is thus approximately $1.50.

Now let's add yarn costs. Cheap wool or wool-mixture yarn (3-ply Persian or "Persian-type," rug, or shag) to cover your 14-inch canvas design area will cost you from $3 to $4.50. The finest 100 percent long-staple Persian wool will cost you approximately $6, so your maximum yarn saving is about $3.

"Aha!" you point out. "Three dollars and that buck and a half add up to $4.50, which is not to be sneezed at these days."

Your time and labor investment, depending on design complexity, will be somewhere in the neighborhood of fifty hours. At coolie wages of $1 an hour, that's about $50, and at today's minimum labor scale of $2.75 per hour for unskilled labor, it's $137.50; skilled labor at a minimal $4 per hour brings the value of your labor to $200!

What kind of arithmetic makes a combined saving of $4.50 for grossly inferior materials justify the investment of $200, $137.50, or even $50 worth of labor?

May I suggest that you've probably spent more than that $4.50 for a couple of tickets to a disappointing movie, or even for a less-than-mediocre late-supper snack after that crummy movie! And you have nothing to show for either expenditure—not even a pleasant memory.

One thing you can count on with needlepoint: if you put the right things into it, it's there for a very, very long time, for all to behold and enjoy. And, unlike the lousy movie and the crummy supper which (ideally) you can forget, if you use inferior materials in needlework, they'll just lie there and dully stare back at you, not letting you forget.

End of arithmetic lesson.

Floor and Table Frames; Other Tools

If you're accustomed to using a needlepoint floor or table frame (I am not), go right ahead and use it. If you haven't used one, don't bother. Just keep your stitching tension even, and you'll do fine.

If you want to try using a frame for the first time, get one that's sturdy but not too heavy, and make sure its surfaces are smooth. There's no percentage in doing an exquisite piece just to have a snag wreck it for you. Be sure you follow the maker's instructions for setting it up and using it.

How do you know whether or not to use a frame? Since it keeps your canvas reasonably rigid, the tension of your stitches can be expected to be fairly even (if you can be patient with the required two-hand system of stitching). What you won't be able to do is fold up your work and stuff it into your workbag if you want to take off anywhere in a hurry or on impulse. You must first remove the stitches, staples, or tacks that fasten your piece securely to the frame, and then replace them when you get back.

If you want mobility, forget the frame and train yourself to keep an even tension (more on this later). Then, if you haven't distorted your canvas while stitching (and I'm sure you won't), proper blocking will probably straighten you right out.

Your tool chest should contain:

1. Scissors. You'll need two pairs—a large, sturdy one to cut canvas and tape, and a small, embroidery-type pair for your needlework. Be sure the small scissors have at least one slender point (for ripping) and that they are sharp. Ordinary needlepoint is pesky to rip; ripping out needlepoint stitchery can set you to grinding your teeth or kicking the cat. Far better to avoid mistakes. Fasten a cord or ribbon or even a strand of yarn to one handle of your small scissors and hang them where you can see them; I wear mine around my neck when I work.

2. Needles. The usual blunt needlepoint needles in several sizes—#18 generally for 3-ply Persian, #20 for one or two plies of Persian yarn, #13 Smyrna for rug and shag yarns. Store them in a large-ish empty pill vial so they'll rattle at the bottom of your workbag and help you find them when you need them and can't see them.

3. Thimble. This is optional. I find it indispensable for hand sewing but hopelessly in the way when I do needlepoint. The combination of a different needle angle and arthritic fingers probably accounts for my dilemma. You'll have to decide this one for yourself.

4. Tweezers. Choose a pair with squared-off ends; they make ripping out a whole lot easier after the stitches have been carefully clipped.

5. Tape measure. Checking up on measurements as you go along can save you much unnecessary grief.

Marking, Cutting, and Preparing Canvas

Having bought canvas and yarn, you're ready to go to work on your first project. The first step will be marking and cutting a suitably sized piece of canvas to work on. First identify the canvas's selvedge (the woven edge, generally with a colored thread through it).* It should always be on the left- and/or right-hand edge of your canvas, just as it is when you're cutting any other fabric; it clues you in to the straight of your material.

Determine the size of the piece of canvas you'll need (margins plus design area) and write those dimensions down somewhere; one measurement is for the area outside the margins and the other is for the design area.

Plot where you're going to cut out the piece you want, using one edge of your canvas for one edge of your project piece; if you can utilize two edges, better still. Whenever you can, use a selvedge for a left- or right-hand edge. This will minimize waste and give you the largest possible uncut piece of leftover canvas for your next project. And please, don't "eyeball" your measurements; use a tape measure. You'll be glad you did, and so will whoever does your blocking.

Mark the outside dimension carefully on your canvas with a permanent, waterproof, fine-point marker. A black "Sharpee," made by Sanford, is a good all-purpose marker to have handy; you'll find this type of pen in almost any stationery or art-supply store.

Put your outside marking line down in the space between canvas threads. Then proceed to cut with heavy, sharp scissors directly on that mark, keeping as nearly as possible in the center of the marked spaces. The straighter your cut edges, the easier they will be to tape.

When you've cut off what you need, roll up and put aside whatever canvas is left over. You'll use it for a multitude of things you haven't thought of yet. (You'll do the same with leftover yarn.) You'll be happily surprised to find that having a library of canvas and yarn leftovers will soon enable you to design a new piece and start it instantly without having to go out to buy anything . . . and you can't beat *that* for savings!

When there's no selvedge on your canvas, as in, perhaps, a center cut, you'll have to decide which is a top edge and which is a "straight" or side edge before you tape any edges.

* *Selvedge*, sometimes spelled *selvage*, is a simple bastardization of *self-edge*.

11

Unravel one horizontal-edge thread and another thread from a vertical edge. Each thread will have waves in it, but the undulations in one will be more pronounced than in the other. The thread that is almost crimped will be the warp thread, which runs up and down (vertically) in the canvas structure, as does the selvedge. Ironically, the warp thread is the straight of the piece. The less wavy one (the woof thread) is the top edge of your piece.

If this seems like a lot to remember, hang on to *warp* as the key word. Remember that when you set up a loom to weave a fabric, you first put on the warp (vertical threads) straight up and down so that you can send the woof threads through the warp horizontally. In the process of weaving, those vertical warp threads become warped. I hope that helps you to remember; it works for me.

Your canvas needs to be bound on all cut edges so that it doesn't ravel. You have a choice of several methods. One way is to use masking or freezer tape (at least 1 inch wide) or any other tape that is adhesive and durable but will not ooze its sticky backing under the warmth of your hands. Keep in mind that the taped edge must survive being handled until the work is completed and laundered and blocked. My own choice is a white muslin-faced industrial adhesive tape.

The tape is laid flat on a table top, adhesive side up; the cut canvas edge is laid on the adhesive side of the tape, parallel to the tape, so that a little less than half of the tape's width is covered by the canvas. Cut the piece of tape from the roll. Lightly smooth down the canvas edge, making sure it adheres to the tape. Starting from the middle of the length of tape, fold the rest of the tape over onto the top of the canvas, covering the length of the canvas edge. Repeat on the other cut edges of canvas. The selvedge doesn't require taping.

Another method requires a sewing machine. Make a zigzag stitch ½ inch in from the edge; fold over on the stitching and do two or three more rows of zigzag stitching back and forth on the folded area.

A third technique is to use white glue (Sobo is best) and glue down a ½-inch hem. Be sure the glue dries thoroughly before you attempt to work on your project.

A good conservative method is to sew a fabric binding at least 1 inch wide on all cut edges, using two or three rows of stitching to secure it.

Needle
Threading

How and when do you start? Any minute now. First I have to tell you about needle threading. There are several ways, all different from the way you thread a needle with cotton thread. One thing that won't help you one iota is moistening the end of the yarn as you might a cotton sewing thread. The wool yarn won't stiffen or hold still; it'll only give you a mouthful of wool fibers!

One way to thread your needle is, in reality, to "needle your thread." About a needle's length away from one end of the strand of yarn, separate the plies of yarn so they lie alongside each other, thus lessening the bulk. Fold the yarn over the eye of the needle and pinch tightly; draw out the needle, still holding the yarn firmly pinched between thumb and forefinger. Then slide the needle's hole or "eye" down over the pinched fold of yarn. Draw the fold up through the eye until the short end of the yarn is pulled through and *voilà!*—your thread has been needled.

An alternate system requires you to cut a strip of paper $\frac{1}{4}$ inch wide and 2 inches long. Bring the narrow ends together and fold (see drawings, next page). Put one end of the yarn inside the folded paper strip so that it's parallel to the long side, slide the fold into the eye of the needle, and pull the paper (and yarn) through; save the paper fold for further use.

If you can't make either of these systems work for you, try a needle threader, which you can probably get at your local needlework shop. They're generally either a very thin flat metal device or a wire loop contraption and sell for about 25 cents apiece. If you're going to use a threader, I suggest you buy a few while you're at it; the mortality rate is fairly high. There are few things more maddening than a rainy Sunday with no needle threader at hand—unless it's a leisurely week in a summer cabin without your needles!

Whatever system you settle on, be sure, when your needle has been threaded, that only about 3 to 4 inches of "tail" is drawn through and that you never work with any tail longer than that. Drawing your needle through the space between meshes always brings along two strands, the long working strand and the shorter tail. If there is already a stitch in that

13

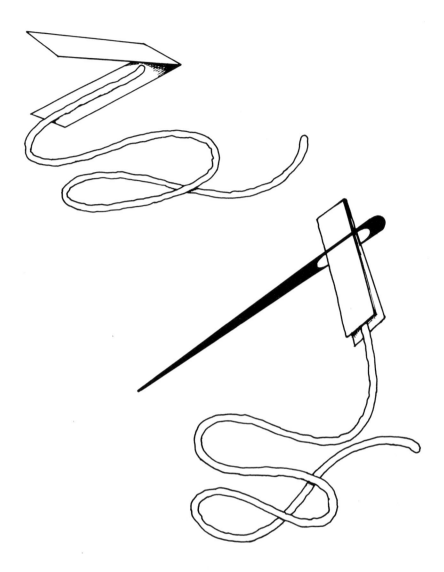

space, the area becomes more congested with two additional strands, thus creating an unavoidable abrasion. What I'm suggesting is that the shorter the tail, the less yarn experiences this super abrasion, the less straining and thinning of the strand, and the less fuzzy the result. A minimal amount of abrasion is inherent in the process of needlework; try to keep it at that minimal level. When you close your hand around your threaded needle, an inch of tail showing below your curled fingers will be a sign that your needle is threaded properly, and that you're exposing the least possible yarn to the abrasion process.

Two Basic Stitches

Before you tackle your first project, there are two basic stitches you need to know: the *continental stitch* and the *basketweave stitch*. Both stitches are basic to needlepoint generally, and you'll need to know them to complete every one of the designs you work up in stitchery. If you don't already know them, now is the time to learn them and get it over with. If you have been doing them, please check out my instructions anyway. You may have a surprise in store for you, after all.

Each is a variation of the tent stitch, that short, 45-degree diagonal stitch which covers a single mesh of canvas, slanting up from lower left to upper right or "from southwest to northeast," or "from Mexico to Maine," whichever locks the direction firmly in your mind.

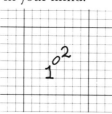

TENT STITCH

The continental stitch, illustrated below and next page, is never, I repeat *never*, to be used as a background stitch, all needlepointers of long experience to the contrary notwithstanding. Heresy, you say—well, perhaps.

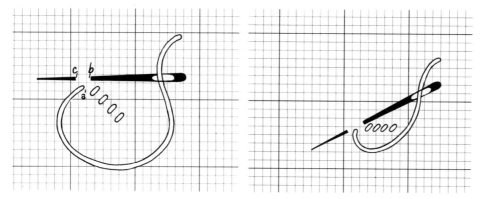

CONTINENTAL STITCH

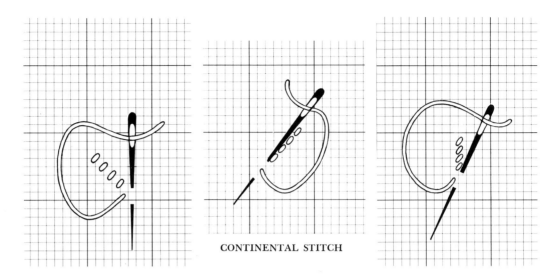

CONTINENTAL STITCH

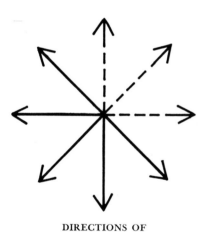

DIRECTIONS OF
CONTINENTAL STITCH

While it's true that generations of needlepointers have used (and still do!) the continental to work back and forth in single horizontal lines across their canvases to fill in solid background areas, the practice should be discouraged by teachers everywhere. The dreadful distortion of the canvas that results can almost never be eradicated by soaking and blocking! If it does appear to be all right, you can bet it's a temporary condition.

Sometimes steaming the back of the work will create a feltlike condition of matted fibers which may give the illusion that the piece has been squared. Not so. What you have produced is a kind of temporary felt which will respond to vagrant humidity, even after being framed or mounted or upholstered, by puckering your canvas as it strains to revert to its original distortion.

The truth of the matter is that in solid areas the continental stitch *always* distorts the canvas, cannot be properly blocked, and creates a corduroy surface totally unacceptable in fine needlepoint. It has survived as a background stitch because it's easy to learn and easy to do; most commercial kits recommend it because it uses yarn economically and is very simple to teach. This is not to say it's useless.

It is an extremely useful stitch—in fact nearly indispensable—as a wheel-horse or steering wheel to get a single line of the design from one place to another. In other words, you should use the continental stitch to travel in any direction *other than* back and forth across the canvas!

The diagonal tent stitch, so called because the rows of tent stitches are worked diagonally across the canvas (see drawing, opposite page), is better known as the basketweave stitch, another error compounded by common usage. In this case the name became popular because the back of the diagonal tent stitch suggests the even weave of basketry. However, even I have to acknowledge that there are some tides you can't buck, and popular usage of basketweave as the name of the stitch seems to be one of them. Throughout this book we shall call the diagonal tent stitch the basketweave stitch. When, later in the book, you come across a *"true"* basketweave stitch, you'll understand my reluctance to make this concession to the pressure of common usage.

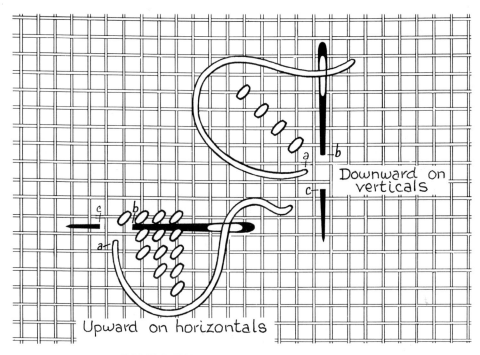

BASKETWEAVE OR DIAGONAL TENT STITCH

Why is it particularly important to learn the basketweave stitch *properly* (read, "by *my* system")? It's important because my system guarantees that the yarn will fit the mesh of the canvas like custom-made gloves, eliminating any possibility of that "dandruff" look some needlepoint pieces have. The stitches will loft with the canvas threads, always creating a smooth, lustrous surface, leaving nothing to chance. With my system you can put your work down, come back to it seven months later (having completely forgotten where you left off and where you were heading), pick up exactly where you stopped, and continue to go your serene way without a hitch or a mistake.

You can even work on your design in five different areas and mesh them all up together without making that giveaway diagonal ridge that looks like a zipper and says you goofed and did two adjoining rows in the same direction.

The system may sound complicated on first reading, but it's no more difficult than learning to tell your right hand from your left and never forgetting the difference.

The important thing to remember about the basketweave stitch is that it is a perfect background stitch—not the only one, by a long shot, but an ideal one for needlepoint. In fact, it should be used in regular needlepoint anywhere that there are two or more rows, however short, of stitches to be done; only if the design moves in a *single* line in any direction should the continental stitch be used. In this way you ensure perfectly aligned blocking of your piece, which in turn ensures perfect fit and surface of the finished article, the end goal of all your energies and efforts and expenditure. Why jeopardize all that when insurance costs nothing?

CONTINENTAL STITCH INSTRUCTIONS

Most people are familiar with the continental stitch only when it is worked in rows moving horizontally to the left (see page 15). Of the eight directions in which tent stitches may be laid down on needlepoint canvas, there are five directions in which the continental stitch may properly and efficiently be worked (see pages 15–16).

The continental stitch is formed when you come up through the canvas at *a* ("Mexico"), go down at *b* ("Maine") and bring the needle up through the canvas again at *c*, ready to start the next stitch. Your needle moves from the left of the mesh to the right, with the needle coming up through the canvas for the next stitch either *diagonally above to the left* of your completed stitch, *horizontally to the left* of it, *diagonally below to the left, directly below,* or *diagonally below to the right* (see page 16).

Depending on which path you're traveling, *c* is apt to be in any one of five places, so I suggest you work carefully and evenly, always pausing to determine where *c* is going to be before plunging in at *b*.

To work in any of the other three directions (see dotted lines in drawing, page 16), you'll need to turn your canvas halfway around so the bottom edge becomes the temporary top edge of your canvas; when you've finished this part of the design, turn the canvas back to its original position and proceed. In any case, the rhythm of forming the stitches remains basically the same.

BASKETWEAVE STITCH INSTRUCTIONS

The basketweave stitch looks somewhat like the continental stitch since, like the continental, it is basically a tent stitch: a slanted stitch that covers a single mesh of canvas at a time, at a 45-degree angle, slanting up from lower left to upper right of the mesh. Structurally, the basketweave is the continental stitch worked diagonally in alternating rows, *down to the right* and *up to the left*. Unlike the continental stitch, however, the basketweave stitch is never worked in a single row; it is always worked in *two* alternating diagonal rows, one upward, the next downward.

The back of the canvas reveals why it's called basketweave stitch, since it suggests a woven basketry pattern; more importantly, it also gives us the clue to why this is such an exemplary stitch. Each changing row direction sets up a perfect counterbalance of tension on the canvas so there can be no distortion. There's ample yarn behind the canvas to provide excellent substance, especially important in upholstered pieces, pillows, clothing, or other covered pieces that will receive frequent wear or handling.

A look at the stitch guide for the basketweave stitch shows that the construction of the stitch is also similar to that of the continental, that is, up at *a*, down at *b*, and up again at *c* (see page 17). In the case of basketweave, *c* is on the *path* that's either upward to the left or downward to the right. More specifically, *c* is, as always, at the lower left of the mesh to be covered.

"The System"

Since the System applies only to monofilament (single-thread) canvas and the basketweave stitch, it might be helpful at this time to examine your canvas a little more closely. You'll find that each mesh (crossed canvas thread) has uppermost either a horizontal or a vertical canvas thread that looks like the drawings on page 6. For brevity's sake, we'll call these meshes horizontals and verticals.

A closer examination will show that you can trace the horizontals in a diagonal row; the verticals will also take a diagonal direction. Checking further, you'll find that each diagonal row of meshes is alternately all-horizontal or all-vertical. Since this is true throughout the entire canvas, the system will apply without exception, no matter how or why or where the path of basketweave stitches is interrupted.

What I propose is that we take full advantage of the grain of the canvas —the way the canvas threads lie in relationship to one another and to the whole canvas.

Adherence to the System on *any* gauge of mono canvas will guarantee a consistently smooth surface with no problem areas and no "corduroy" or "zipper" lines. Each stitch will be beautifully lofted, and, assuming your needle is threaded with the necessary number of plies for the gauge of canvas you're using, your meshes will be completely covered.

In needlepoint, when an infinitesimal area of each mesh is inadequately covered by the yarn, the resultant telltale "dandruff" look can be especially maddening because it only asserts itself in a cumulative way; you can almost never spot it happening until long after it has happened! By that time, as any veteran needlepointer will bear witness, you've gone too far to want to rip back, there really isn't enough room for sneaking in another ply, and if you do shove another one in, you'll find you've brought on yourself that old familiar "cake and milk" syndrome, where nothing ever evens itself out satisfactorily.

You're probably wondering why the "dandruff" look shows up in some places on pieces you or others have worked and is totally absent in other places. This happens because there were times when, by sheer accident, you've all used my system but didn't realize you had; in other places and at other times, you missed it completely because you were probably unaware of the existence of *any* system, let alone mine.

Well, you can now relax in the knowledge that from now on, your basketweave stitch will be a thing of beauty, a joy forever, for here's the System at last.

Basketweave, with or without a system, is worked in alternating diagonal rows in only two directions, one row *upward to the left* of the area, the next row *downward to the right*. The System dictates that *all horizontal mesh must be worked only on an upward row; all verticals are worked only on a downward path*. The System applies everywhere on a canvas; even if a diagonal row consists of only two stitches, you will go upward on horizontals, downward on verticals.

Whenever you're faced with a vertical mesh, you know you're in a downward-moving row; you should therefore look up the diagonal row of bare verticals to find the uppermost or first vertical in that row in order to make your first stitch on the downward path. Similarly, when you see a horizontal mesh, you know you're going to have to find the lowest horizontal for a starting place—when you're working upward, you have to have a place from which to go up.

The System allows you greater freedom to work more relaxedly and thus effortlessly to produce higher-quality work—but only as consistently as the System is used. My hope is that the System will become so much second nature for you that, whenever you pick up a piece of mono canvas to do the basketweave stitch, you'll immediately identify the horizontals and verticals and start the System right off without even knowing you've done it.

The System, by the way, has a terrific built-in check and double-check to keep you out of trouble; when you're holding your needle horizontally ($\longleftrightarrow$) to work an upward row, if you're on the beam, you should be covering horizontal mesh only (see page 6). If you're making a downward diagonal path with your needle held vertically ($\updownarrow$), you should be covering vertical mesh only (see page 6). At the end of each row, after you've done the last stitch in that row, your needle should be angled, rather than horizontal ($\longleftrightarrow$) or vertical ($\updownarrow$), in order to put the needle's point in place for the first stitch of the next row.

A note of caution: Double-check at the end of each row that the last stitch is exactly where you want it to be, and that the first stitch of the new row is clearly in the right place. The place that gives nearly everyone trouble when first beginning is on the right-hand side at the end of a down row, so watch it. Try not to make the omission, but if you do, correct it at once, while there's little to rip back. For your own sake, *don't fudge it; correct it.*

You expect your doctor, your plumber, even your hairdresser to work painstakingly and conscientiously; why not join me and the rest of the nearly vanished species who believe in and insist on quality standards in every detail, in their own work as well as in the work of others?

Tension and Body Rhythms

Had a fight with father, mother, sister, brother, friend, husband, or lover? I hope you resolve it . . . because if you don't, your rage will simply transfer itself to your handwork until the storm is dissipated; let someone or something remind you and it all rises to the surface of your needlepoint once again.

What's to be done about it? Well, you've several alternatives. You can put your work away until a better day comes along; you can go finish up the fight; you can limp along as the victim of an unresolved conflict, uptight and unseeing and botching up your work with uneven tension. Or you can assess what's going on and resolve to keep it out of your work.

If you opt for self-determination, make it easy for yourself by creating as pleasant an ambiance as you can for working. First find a really comfortable place to sit—perhaps in bed, or in the guest room, perhaps at the dining room table so you can spread everything out, perhaps cross-legged on the floor with all your paraphernalia on the sofa. What's really important is that if you're going to make a try for any relaxation of your tension, you need to give yourself every break, physically. You need a comfortable seat, a comfortable work space, and good, consistent light.

If the time and the place are right, you can calm down and do a therapeutic number on yourself by slipping as quickly as possible into your own normal, naturally relaxed, body rhythm. Once you've latched onto your regular body rhythm, your immersion in your handwork will take over and all those tight places in you will just "ease on down the road" all by themselves. How? Simple.

Just do some practice basketweave stitching on a piece of scrap canvas for a few minutes. Concentrate on getting the yarn just to lie on the canvas without moving or distorting the canvas threads. When you can do this consistently, you're into your own body rhythm and you're ready to go to work.

21

What's a body rhythm? And what's so special about having your own?

Well, your body has hundreds of habits that form their own special rhythms, most of them generally unknown to you until you start to check them out. For instance, the way you pick up your fork and knife, the way you brush your hair, the way you approach putting on your sweater, or the way you handle your needle when you sew your stitches into the canvas— have you ever really noticed how you do them?

Jennie, with every stroke, points her needle toward her left shoulder; her sister pulls her needle through the canvas aiming directly at her navel, hesitates, and smoothly shifts direction toward her left hip. Mrs. H. takes her needle on a parabolic swing toward her right shoulder and slides past her right ear. Lore comes straight up from the canvas. Some draw the needle and yarn completely through the canvas with one long, full stroke; some stop when three-quarters of the yarn has been quickly drawn through and then, catching the yarn where it's coming through the canvas, pull the rest through very slowly. Some bring needle and yarn through the canvas about 4 or 5 inches, then draw out the rest of the yarn in several additional short pulls.

I was astonished at the number of different body rhythms I observed among my students. What was even more shocking was to realize how completely unconscious little ol' observant teacher was about her own body rhythms. I'd been needlepointing about six years before I realized that when I do a descending row of basketweave I hold my needle vertically, but when I do the next row (an ascending row), instead of holding my needle horizontally, as I teach it, I automatically turn my canvas a quarter-turn to the left. In effect, I'm now working on a descending row again (this time from the right) and I continue to hold my needle vertically in an unconscious effort to maintain the same body rhythm and to continue holding my needle vertically without interruption.

The moral of this particular little tale is that you are best served by allowing your own special body rhythm to dictate how you sew on your canvas. Your body instinctively finds the way you can most comfortably and easily accomplish what you want to do—so let it. Trying to force new movements will inevitably create new tensions and problems, so cool it, relax, and enjoy.

General Directions

1. Before you start to work, read all instructions and examine the black-and-white detail photograph (one-quarter of the finished work), the symbol guide, the stitch guides, and, of course, the graph, which shows you where all those stitches go.

2. To find the center of the canvas, first fold the canvas in half lengthwise and then crosswise; mark where the folds meet with a safety pin or basting thread. This will match the center space or mesh shown by a large arrowhead on the graph.

3. The graph shows the upper right-hand quarter of the design. Each background line on the graph represents one thread of mono canvas (the same line equals two threads of Penelope canvas). There is no need to mark the placement of stitches on the canvas itself; simply refer to the graph and count threads.

4. Unless otherwise specified, start from the center and work each stitch pattern until its area is completed in all four sections of the canvas. Before starting each stitch pattern, check your graph. Some stitch patterns go around corners while others stop at the corner to change direction and then go on to the next corner. Before starting a new stitch pattern, be sure the preceding stitch area is completed.

5. When working with two plies of Persian yarn, remove one ply from the center section of a 3-ply strand and pair it up with a single ply drawn from another 3-ply strand. You now have three 2-ply strands to work with before you need to make any more—a small time saver, but such shortcuts add up in a hurry, and every little bit helps.

6. Begin to needlepoint by holding the end of the yarn at the back of the canvas until several stitches have been worked to cover it. To begin and end each successive strand, weave the yarn horizontally (⟷) or vertically (↕) (*never* diagonally) under stitches on the back of your work for at least 1 inch. Cautiously cut the yarn close to the canvas.

7. One last admonition seems in order: *never,* unless you have no choice, bring your needle up through the canvas in a space already occupied by yarn. Instead, make a point of coming up through *bare canvas* and put your needle very precisely *down* into any occupied space. Be especially careful not to split or disturb the yarn that already occupies that space; your reward will be immediate—and permanent.

Designs and Projects

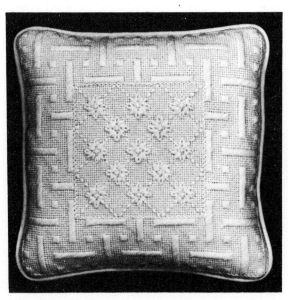

Chinoiserie

Design area approximately 10½ inches square (add margins)
#12 mono canvas
150 short (30-inch) strands Persian yarn (color #010)
See *symbol guide* for stitch symbols and number of plies of yarn.

Special Note: Some of the stitches on this graph go beyond the center mark; take them into account and proceed accordingly.

STARFLOWER STITCH #2. Work starflower first.

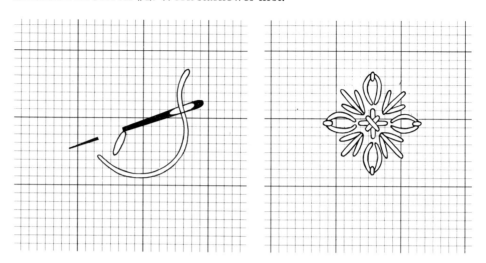

LAZY DAISY STITCH. Hold loop down with free thumb until needle is drawn up through canvas *inside* loop, release thumb, and tie loop down.

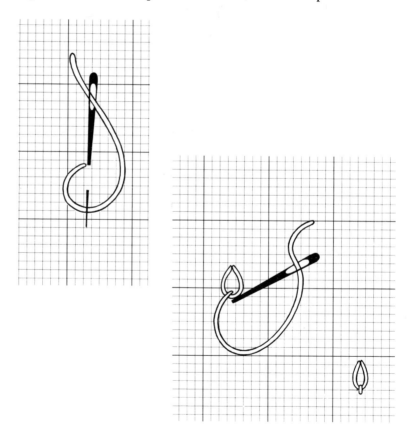

BASKETWEAVE STITCH (page 17). Since the basketweave stitch is generally worked from the top of an area downward, you may, at times, need to turn your canvas halfway around so the bottom edge becomes the temporary top edge of your canvas. When you've finished this part of the design, turn the canvas back to its original position and proceed.

BACKSTITCH. This stitch must follow basketweave to be effective.

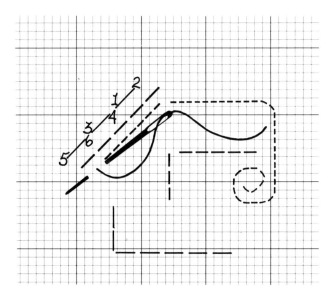

OUTLINE STITCH. Stitch reaches over three canvas threads (*not* mesh), back under one; be careful not to distort canvas threads. This stitch should follow basketweave and slanted Gobelin for better symmetry.

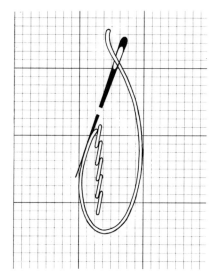

SLANTED (OBLIQUE) GOBELIN STITCH. This stitch is four threads high and four threads wide; the strokes are somewhat lengthy and frequently have a tendency to be too loose. Be watchful and keep the strokes close to the canvas without distorting the canvas threads. Your yarn will kink up from time to time; drop your needle and let the yarn unwind itself. Complete the entire row before working the outline stitches on either side.

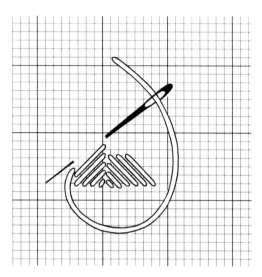

SCOTCH STITCH. The long middle stroke is apt to sag a little unless drawn a trifle more closely; keep units square and even as you work.

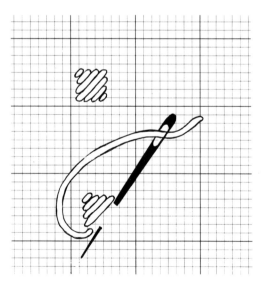

BASKETWEAVE STITCH (page 17). The last two rows are for use by pillow maker, framer, or upholsterer for finishing (see graph).

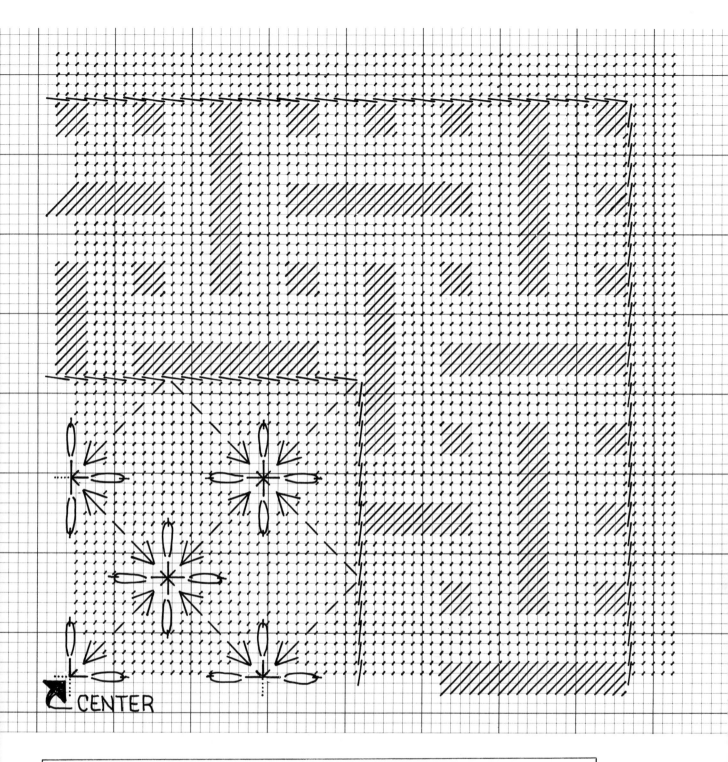

CENTER

Stitch	No. of Plies	Stitch	No. of Plies
Starflower stitch #2	2	Outline stitch	2
Lazy daisy stitch	2	Slanted (oblique) Gobelin stitch	2
Basketweave stitch	2	Scotch stitch	2
Backstitch	2		

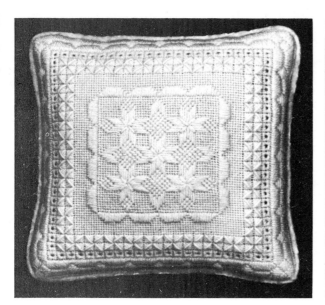
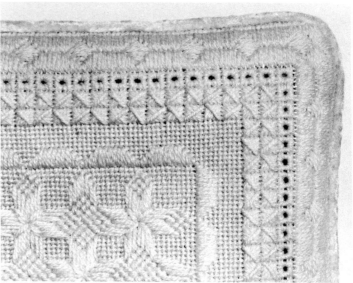

Colonial

Design area approximately 10 inches square (add margins)
#12 mono canvas
110 short (30-inch) strands Persian yarn (color #010)
See *symbol guide* for stitch symbols and number of plies of yarn.

Special Note: Some of the stitches on this graph go beyond the center mark; take them into account and proceed accordingly.

SATIN STITCH MOTIF #1 (A). Note variance in sections *A, B, C, D,* and *E* on the graph. Keep checking graph for directional changes. Keep stitches fairly loose but close to canvas; don't allow them to sag.

TIE-DOWN STITCH. Twist strand of yarn about ten times to tighten. Retwist as necessary.

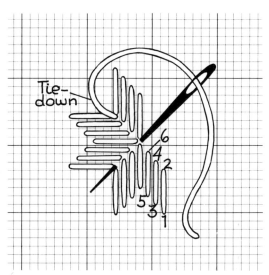

UPRIGHT STITCH. This stitch is best worked in diagonal rows, moving upward to the left and downward to the right.

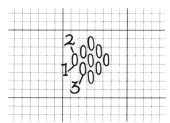

BASKETWEAVE STITCH (page 17). Since the basketweave stitch is generally worked from the top of an area downward, you may, at times, need to turn your canvas halfway around so the bottom edge becomes the temporary top edge of your canvas. When you've finished this part of the design, turn the canvas back to its original position and proceed.

SATIN STITCH B. Check graph for pattern and changes in direction; follow graph carefully.

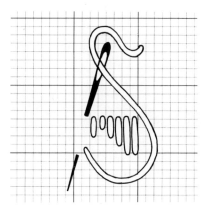

SCOTCH STITCH, REVERSED AND TIED DOWN. Check graph for variations in direction of Scotch stitch. For tie-down, twist yarn about ten times and re-twist as necessary.

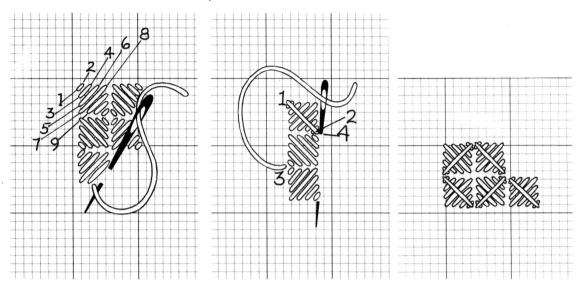

ALGERIAN SQUARE EYELET. To form eyelet properly, yarn tension must be controlled. When making the stitches on each side, pull firmly; release tension on yarn to make corner stitches. Keep eyelet centers uniform in size.

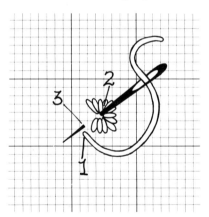

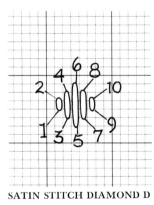

SATIN STITCH DIAMOND D

SATIN STITCH C. See graph for pattern and changes of direction; follow graph carefully.

SATIN STITCH DIAMOND (D). See graph for pattern and changes of direction; follow graph carefully.

SATIN STITCH E. See graph for pattern and changes of direction; follow graph carefully.

BASKETWEAVE STITCH (page 17). The last two rows are for use by pillow maker, framer, or upholsterer for finishing (see graph).

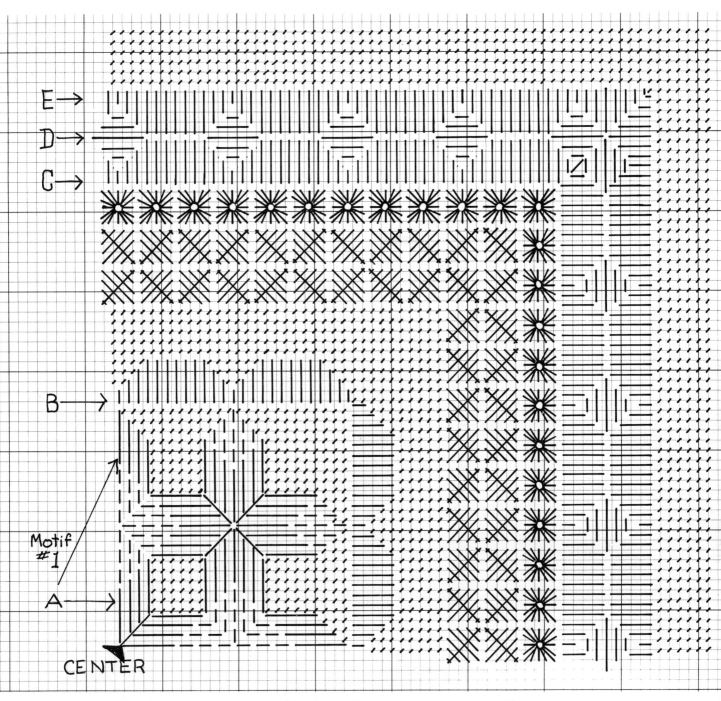

	Stitch	No. of Plies		Stitch	No. of Plies
	Satin stitch motif #1	3		Satin stitch	3
				Scotch stitch, reversed and tied down	2
	Tie-down stitch	3		Algerian square eyelet	2
	Upright stitch	3		Satin stitch diamond	3
	Basketweave stitch	2			

Diamond Quilt

Design area approximately 18 inches square (add margins)
#5 French Penelope canvas
Approximately 14 ounces Pat-Rug yarn (color #010), *not*
including yarn for cord and tassels
Cord: 23 (continuous) yards of rug yarn (color #010)
Tassels: 11½ (continuous) yards of rug yarn (color #010)
4 3-ply strands (30-inch) Persian yarn (color #010)
See *symbol guide* for stitch symbols.

Special Note: Some of the stitches on this graph go beyond the center mark; take them into account and proceed accordingly.

WEB STITCH, WRAPPED. Web must be worked first. Anchor rug yarn securely to canvas, place spokes from outside to center of web. Then, using fresh strand of securely anchored rug yarn, proceed to make seven rows of wrapping, going *back over* one spoke and *forward under* two, and so on.

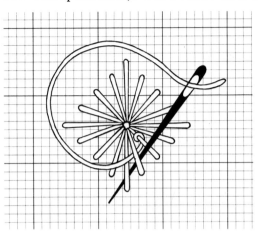

BASKETWEAVE STITCH (page 17). Since the basketweave stitch is generally worked from the top of an area downward, you may, at times, need to turn your canvas halfway around so the bottom edge becomes the temporary top edge of your canvas. When you've finished this part of the design, turn the canvas back to its original position and proceed.

SMYRNA CROSS-STITCH. Follow the same sequence of construction throughout project, that is, the diagonal cross first, then an upright cross. Finish with the horizontal stroke on top as your last stroke before proceeding to the next Smyrna cross-stitch.

BASKETWEAVE STITCH. See page 17.

SCOTCH STITCH, REVERSED. The long middle stroke is apt to sag a little unless you draw it a trifle more closely; don't distort canvas threads. Keep checking graph for direction changes.

TIE-DOWN STITCH. Twist strand five times. Retwist as necessary.

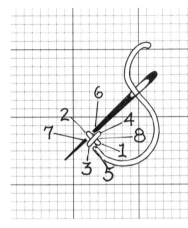

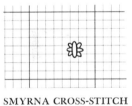

SMYRNA CROSS-STITCH

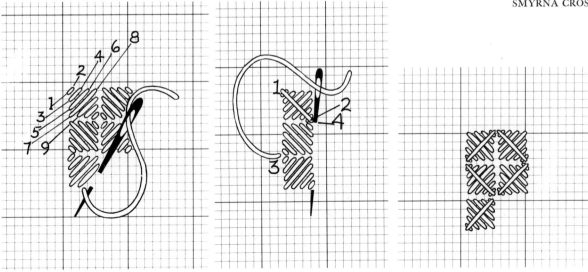

SHEAF STITCH. Watch your tension; let the five strokes of each stitch just lie on the canvas. The tie-down stroke, when drawn into place, should cover two threads of canvas. Check graph and note that outer strokes of each sheaf share spaces with those of following sheaves.

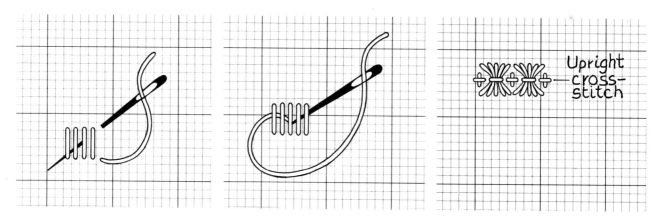

UPRIGHT CROSS-STITCH. Complete each upright cross-stitch before going on to the next; *all* top strokes of stitches should be horizontal.

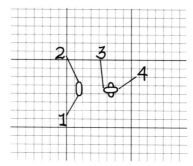

SLANTED (OBLIQUE) GOBELIN STITCH. There are eight sections of this stitch; check graph for directional changes. This stitch is four threads high and four threads wide, so the strokes are somewhat lengthy and frequently have a tendency to be too loose. Be watchful and keep the strokes close to the canvas without distorting the canvas threads. Your yarn will kink up from time to time; drop your needle and let the yarn unwind itself.

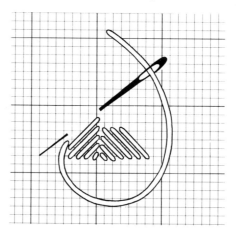

BASKETWEAVE STITCH. See page 17.

SMYRNA CROSS-STITCH, REVERSED. Follow the same sequence of construction throughout the project; make upright cross-stitch first, then top with diagonal cross-stitch, completing each Smyrna before going on to the next stitch. Be sure *all* top stitches slant in the same direction.

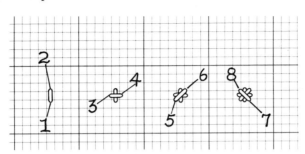

BASKETWEAVE STITCH (page 17). These two rows are for use by pillow maker, framer, or upholsterer for finishing (see graph, next page).

TWISTED CORD (requires two people). Fold a 23-yard strand of yarn in four; make an overhand knot at each end. Each person slips a pencil into the loop at one end and, holding yarn loosely just below the pencil with one hand, twists the pencil with the other hand. *Extremely important*: both persons twist pencils clockwise, holding the yarn absolutely taut until it begins to kink; catch center over a doorknob or hook. Then bring pencils together for one person to hold, while the other transfers one end loop, leaving both loops on one pencil. Remove twisted yarn from doorknob and hold twist at center. Sliding one hand down yarn toward this end and releasing it at short intervals, let yarn twist by itself. Secure each knot separately by winding sewing thread where twist stops. Fasten off with a few knotted stitches. Trim ends off evenly.

TASSELS. Make four twisted cords using the technique above; use one 30-inch (3-ply) strand of Persian yarn for each. For each tassel cut 40 10-inch strands of rug yarn. Fold the twisted Persian yarn cord in half; place center of tassel pieces across doubled cord near loop end. Draw cord ends over tassel strands and through loop; pull tightly. Holding all tassel ends together, wrap a piece of Persian yarn three or four times around the whole bunch, about 1 inch from folded end of rug yarn tassel; knot securely. Trim tassel ends.

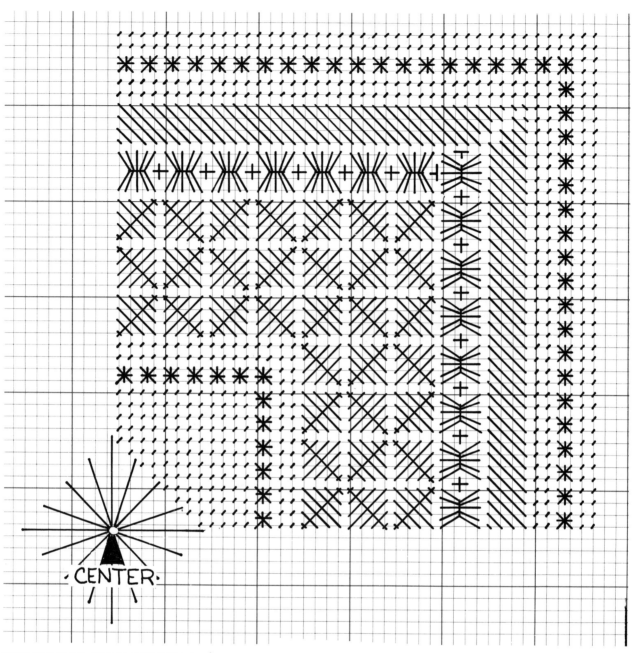

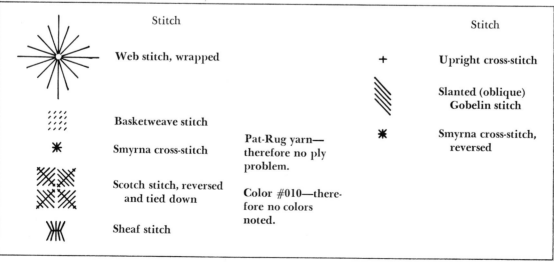

	Stitch			Stitch
	Web stitch, wrapped		+	Upright cross-stitch
	Basketweave stitch			Slanted (oblique) Gobelin stitch
*	Smyrna cross-stitch	Pat-Rug yarn— therefore no ply problem.	✳	Smyrna cross-stitch, reversed
	Scotch stitch, reversed and tied down	Color #010—there-fore no colors noted.		
	Sheaf stitch			

Diamond Web Pincushion

The finished project is shown in Plate 2.

Design area approximately 5 inches square (add margins)
#5 French Penelope canvas
Pat-Rug yarn: #424, 5 long (60-inch) strands
Persian yarn: #424, 12 short (30-inch) strands; #434, 23 short
(30-inch) strands
See *symbol guide* for stitch symbols, colors, and number of plies of yarn.

WEB STITCH, WRAPPED. Anchor rug yarn firmly for base strokes at beginning and end of web. Start to wrap with fresh long strand after anchoring it securely. It will take at least six rows of wrapping with extra wrapping required at points; go *back over* one spoke, *forward under* two, and so on.

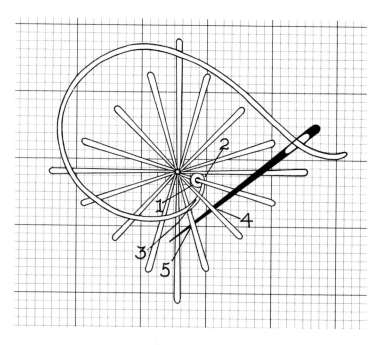

BASKETWEAVE STITCH (page 17). Since the basketweave stitch is generally worked from the top of an area downward, you may, at times, need to turn your canvas halfway around so the bottom edge becomes the temporary top edge of your canvas. When you've finished this part of the design, turn the canvas back to its original position and proceed. Separate canvas threads so that you can stitch over single mesh (ten to the inch instead of five) and follow graph for placement, using Persian yarn. Fill in exposed canvas between spokes of web, even if not shown on graph.

SMYRNA CROSS-STITCH. Using Persian yarn (check *symbol guide* for color and plies), make diagonal cross first, then top with upright cross, completing each Smyrna before going on to the next stitch. Be sure *all* top strokes are horizontal.

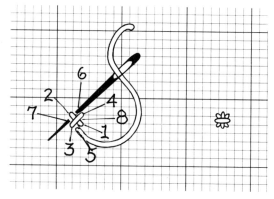

BASKETWEAVE STITCH (page 17). The last two rows are for use in finishing (see graph).

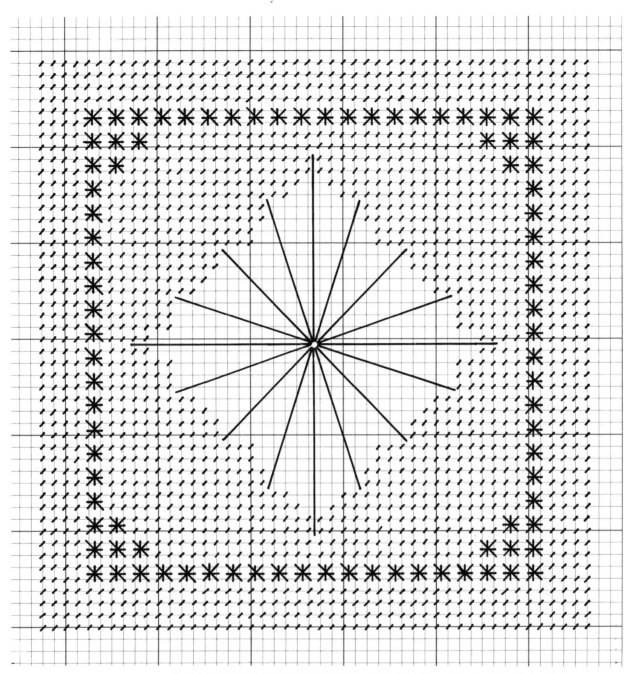

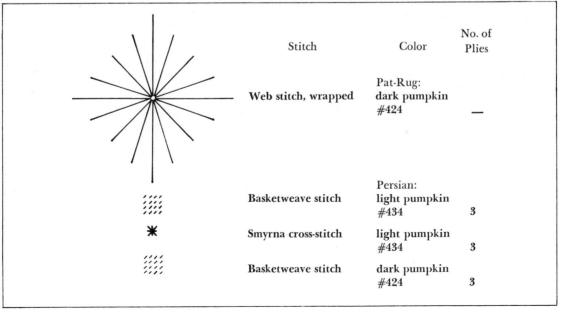

	Stitch	Color	No. of Plies
	Web stitch, wrapped	Pat-Rug: dark pumpkin #424	—
	Basketweave stitch	Persian: light pumpkin #434	3
	Smyrna cross-stitch	light pumpkin #434	3
	Basketweave stitch	dark pumpkin #424	3

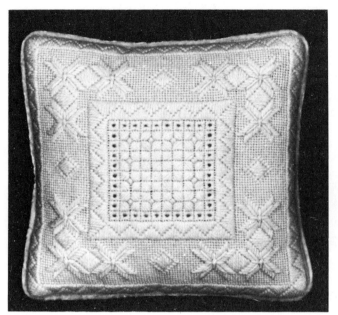

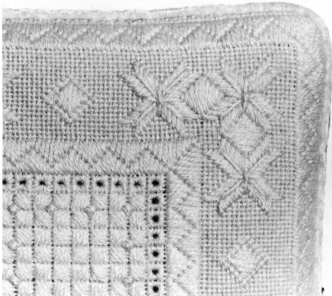

Federal

Design area approximately 10 inches square (add margins)
#12 mono canvas
110 short (30-inch) strands Persian yarn (color #010)
See *symbol guide* for stitch symbols and number of plies of yarn.

Special Note: Some of the stitches on this graph go beyond the center mark; take them into account and proceed accordingly.

SCOTCH STITCH, REVERSED. Check graph for changes in direction of stitch.

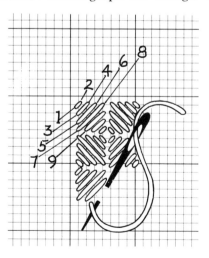

KNOTTED UPRIGHT CROSS-STITCH. Check graph for placement. It is essential to form the vertical stroke *first* so horizontal can hold it down. *All* top strokes slant in same direction.

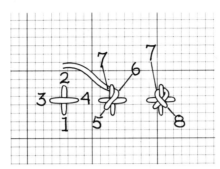

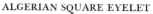

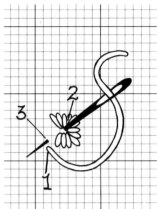

ALGERIAN SQUARE EYELET. To keep outer edges of eyelet square, yarn tension must be controlled. When making side stitches, pull tightly; release tension on yarn to make corner stitches. All strokes are formed from outer edges of eyelet toward inner spaces. Keep eyelet centers uniform in size.

SATIN STITCH A. Note sections *A*, *B*, and *C* on the graph. Watch for variations in satin stitch patterns and follow the graph carefully.

BASKETWEAVE STITCH (page 17). Since the basketweave stitch is generally worked from the top of an area downward, you may, at times, need to turn your canvas halfway around so the bottom edge becomes the temporary top edge of your canvas. When you've finished this part of the design, turn the canvas back to its original position and proceed.

SATIN STITCH MOTIF #2 (B). Check graph for section *B* patterns.

TIE-DOWN STITCH. Twist yarn five times to tighten. Retwist as necessary.

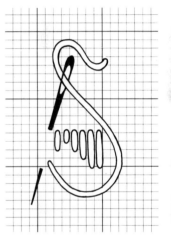

SATIN STITCH A

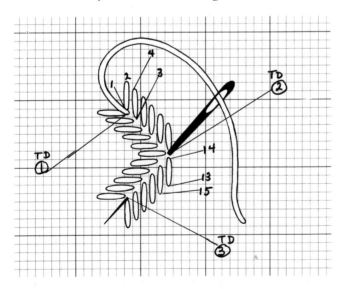

KNOTTED UPRIGHT CROSS-STITCH. See above.

SATIN STITCH C. Check graph section *C* for patterns.

BASKETWEAVE STITCH (page 17). The last two rows are for use by pillow maker, framer, or upholsterer for finishing (see graph, next page).

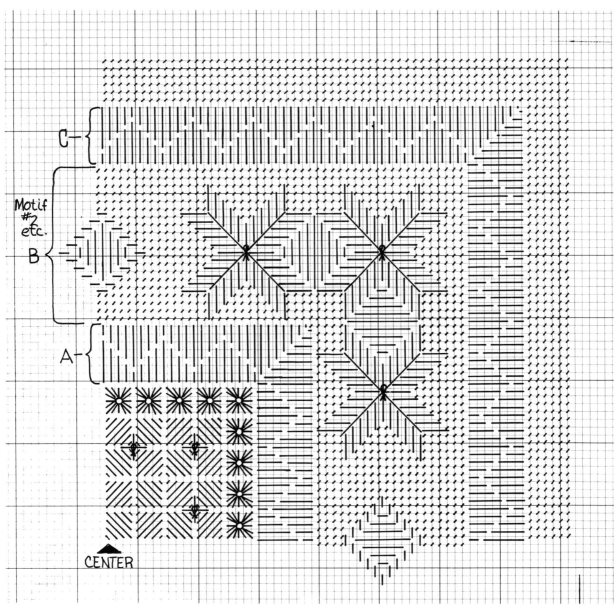

	Stitch	No. of Plies		Stitch	No. of Plies
	Scotch stitch, reversed	2		Satin stitch motif #2	3
	Knotted upright cross-stitch	3		Tie-down stitch	3
	Algerian square eyelet	2		Satin stitch	3
	Satin stitch	3			
	Basketweave stitch	2			

Focus

The finished project is shown in Plate 3.

Design area approximately 14½ inches square (add margins)
#5 French Penelope canvas
Pat-Rug yarn: 2 ounces each #455, #453, #433; 5 ounces #445
See *symbol guide* for stitch symbols and colors.

Special Note: Some of the stitches on this graph go beyond the center mark; take them into account and proceed accordingly.

WEB STITCH, WRAPPED. The web must be worked first. Anchor rug yarn securely to canvas, placing spokes from outside to center of web; then, using fresh strand of securely anchored rug yarn, proceed to make five rows of wrapping going *back over* one spoke and *forward under* two, and so on.

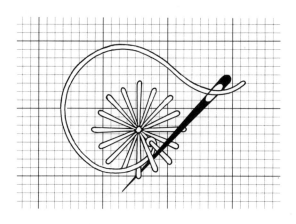

BASKETWEAVE STITCH (page 17). Since the basketweave stitch is generally worked from the top of an area downward, you may, at times, need to turn your canvas halfway around so the bottom edge becomes the temporary top edge of your canvas. When you've finished this part of the design, turn the canvas back to its original position and proceed.

SMYRNA CROSS-STITCH. Follow the same sequence of construction throughout project, that is, a diagonal cross first, then an upright cross, finishing with the horizontal stroke on top as your last stroke before proceeding to the next Smyrna cross-stitch.

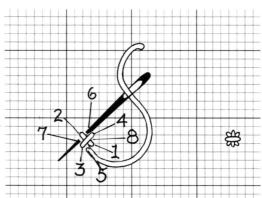

SCOTCH STITCH, VARIATION 1. Do basketweave half first, then finish with Scotch stitch half, beginning with long stroke, which partially covers preceding stitches; don't allow the long stroke to sag.

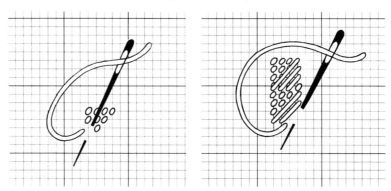

WOVEN CROSS-STITCH. Place the four strokes of this stitch in the same order each time, being careful when you make your last stroke to weave through the previous strokes without going into the canvas.

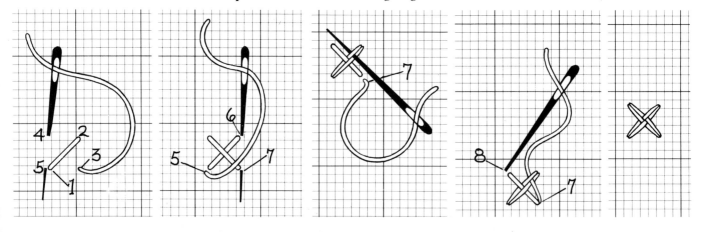

CONTINENTAL STITCH AND REVERSE (pages 15–16). These few little stitches with the big name are simply background fill-in stitches to cover exposed canvas; see graph for placement.

FRENCH KNOT STITCH. This should be a fairly large, somewhat loose knot, since it's formed in a single space and you don't want it to slide through when you draw it together.

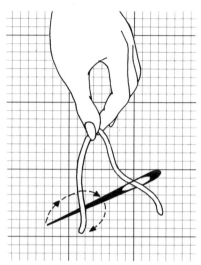

CASHMERE STITCH. Note that this stitch is done in two different directions; check your graph.

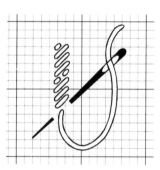

SMYRNA CROSS-STITCH. Check for color change.

SCOTCH STITCH, VARIATION 2. The *incomplete* Scotch stitch strokes must be done first. When they are all in place, do the second half of the stitch; check graph. Don't allow the long stroke to sag.

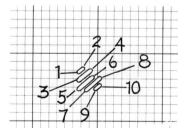 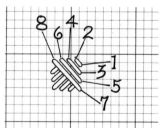

BASKETWEAVE STITCH (page 17). The last two rows are for use by pillow maker, framer, or upholsterer for finishing (see graph, next page).

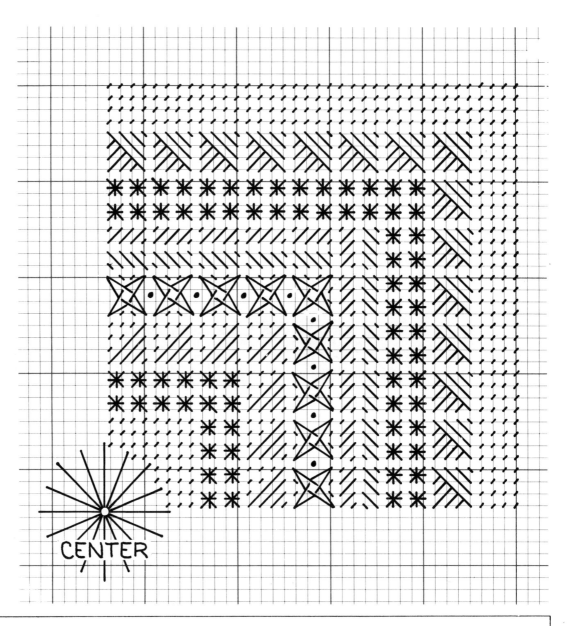

CENTER

Four shades gold, lightest to darkest:
(1) #455, (2) #453, (3) #445, (4) #433

	Stitch	Color		Stitches	Color
	Web stitch, wrapped	4		Continental stitch and reverse	2
				French knot stitch	2
	Basketweave stitch	3		Cashmere stitch	4
	Smyrna cross-stitch	2		Smyrna cross-stitch	3
	Scotch stitch, variation 1	1		Scotch stitch, variation 2	2 first 1 on top
	Woven cross-stitch	3		Basketweave stitch	3

Pat-Rug yarn, therefore no list
of plies needed.

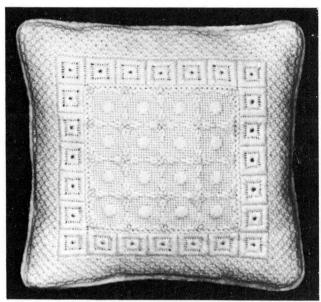

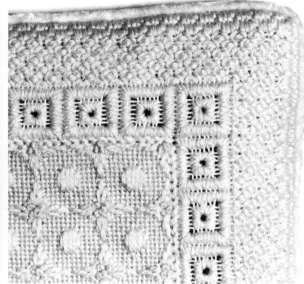

Greek Revival

Design area approximately 10 inches square (add margins)
#12 mono canvas
130 short (30-inch) strands Persian yarn (color #010)
See *symbol guide* for stitch symbols and number of plies of yarn.

Special Note: Some of the stitches on this graph go beyond the center mark; take them into account and proceed accordingly.

STARFLOWER STITCH #1. Starflower must be completed *before* French knots are stitched.

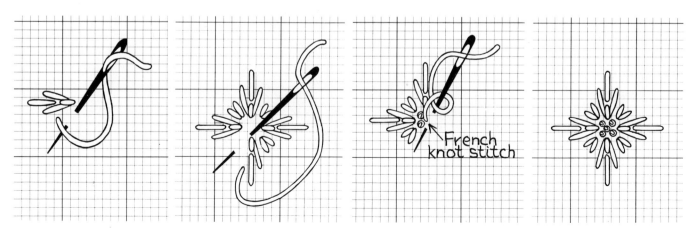

FRENCH KNOT STITCH. Yarn is held taut while stitch is formed.

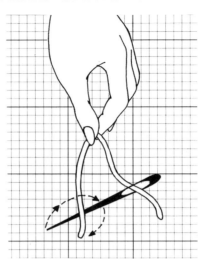

BASKETWEAVE STITCH (page 17). Since the basketweave stitch is generally worked from the top of an area downward, you may, at times, need to turn your canvas halfway around so the bottom edge becomes the temporary top edge of your canvas. When you've finished this part of the design, turn the canvas back to its original position and proceed.

SATIN STITCH A. Note variations of sections *A* and *B* in satin stitch patterns on the graph; follow patterns carefully.

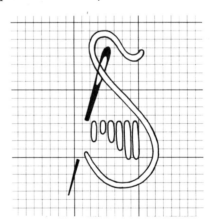

BACKSTITCH. The rhythm of this stitch (over two threads) is similar to the rhythm of continental stitch; keep tension relaxed.

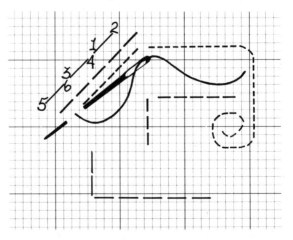

OUTLINE STITCH. Stitch is generally worked *after* the stitches on either side of it are finished; in this instance, finish the backstitch and Algerian super eyelet first. Note that stitch reaches *forward over* three mesh and *back under* one. Check graph for placement.

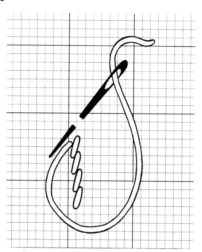

ALGERIAN SUPER EYELET. To keep outer edges of the inner eyelet square, pull yarn firmly toward you when working center stitches of each side, more loosely when working corner stitches; keep eyelet centers uniform in size. Use same tension system when working second half of super eyelet; keep inner and outer edges of second half straight and square, without distorting canvas threads.

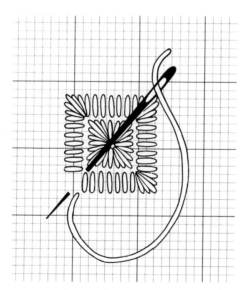

LATTICE STITCH. Work upward and downward in horizontal rows.

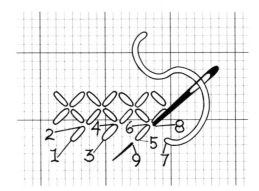

UPRIGHT CROSS-STITCH. Complete each upright cross-stitch before going on to next; work rows upward and downward, diagonally. *All* top strokes of stitches should be horizontal.

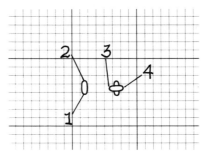

SATIN STITCH B. Check section *B* on graph for patterns; follow graph carefully.

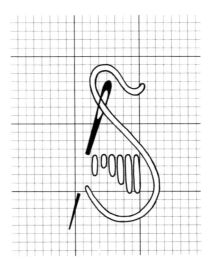

TIE-DOWN STITCH (for similar use see Colonial, page 30). Used only on corners.

BASKETWEAVE STITCH (page 17). Last two rows are for use by pillow maker, framer, or upholsterer for finishing (see graph).

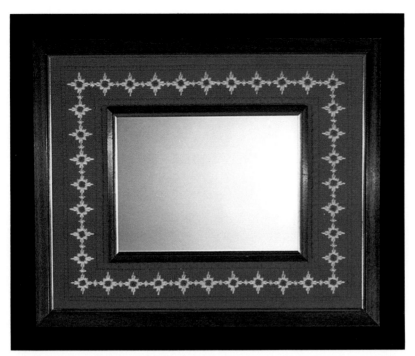

PLATE 1. Red Mirror Frame, as shown in
McCall's Needlework & Crafts Magazine

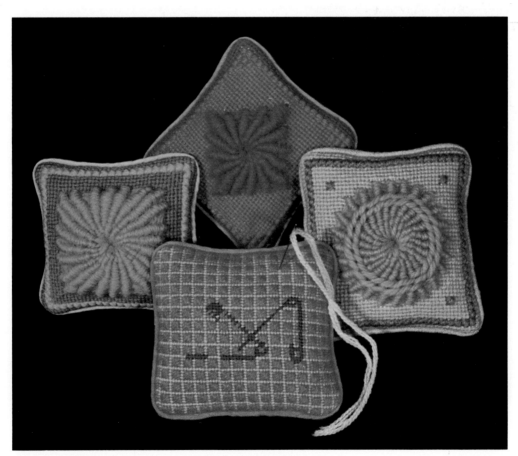

PLATE 2. Clockwise from top: Diamond Web Pincushion,
Round Web Pincushion, Pincushion for Baby,
Square Web Pincushion

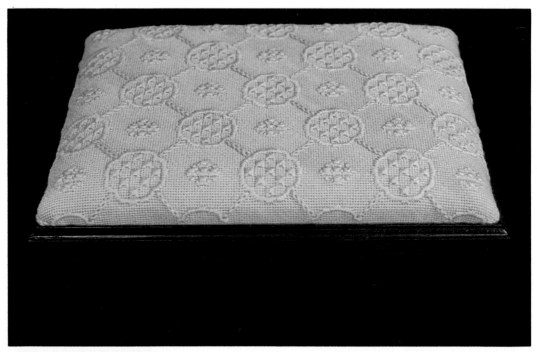

PLATE 4. Ming-Gold Footstool

PLATE 3. Focus

PLATE 5. Naked Blue

PLATE 6. Orange Sherbet

PLATE 8. Texas Star

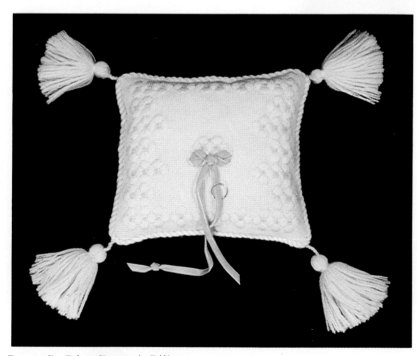

PLATE 7. Ring Bearer's Pillow

PLATE 9. Up, Up, and Away!

PLATE 10. The Notebook, showing some experimental "doodling" in stitchery, some stitches ready to mount, and a few sample pages of stitches and guides already mounted

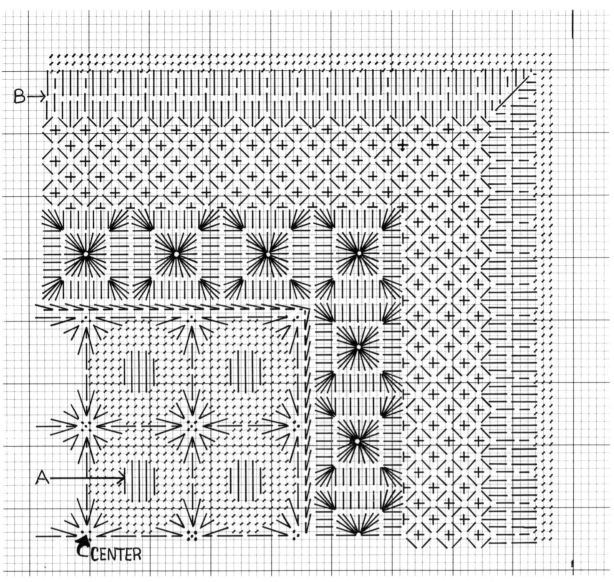

	Stitch	No. of Plies		Stitch	No. of Plies
	Starflower stitch #1	2		Algerian super eyelet	2
	French knot stitch	2			
	Basketweave stitch	2		Lattice stitch	2
	Satin stitch	3	+	Upright cross-stitch	3
	Backstitch	2		Tie-down stitch	3
	Outline stitch	2			

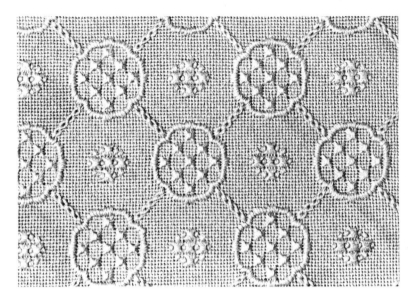

Ming-Gold Footstool

The finished project is shown in Plate 4.

Design area approximately 16½ inches × 12 inches (add margins)
#12 mono canvas
Approximately 280 short (30-inch) strands Persian yarn (color #440)
See *symbol guide* for stitch symbols and number of plies of yarn.

Special Note: Some of the stitches on this graph go beyond the center mark; take into account and proceed accordingly.

SHEAF STITCH. *Important:* Sheaf stitch in this project is worked both horizontally and vertically; check graph before proceeding. Watch your tension; let the five strokes of each stitch just lie on the canvas. The tie-down stroke, when drawn into place, should cover two threads of canvas.

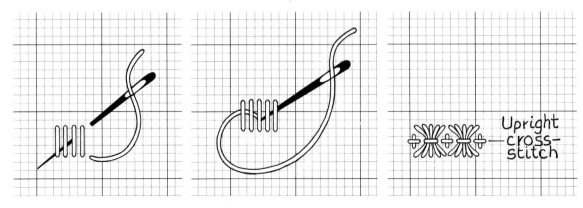

Upright cross-stitch

BASKETWEAVE STITCH (page 17). Since the basketweave stitch is generally worked from the top of an area downward, you may, at times, need to turn your canvas halfway around so the bottom edge becomes the temporary top edge of your canvas. When you've finished this part of the design, turn the canvas back to its original position and proceed.

SATIN STITCH. Carefully follow medallion on graph only *after* basketweave and sheaf stitch centers are worked. Work evenly; leave room for trapunto filling.

TRAPUNTO FILLING. Thread needle with a 3-ply strand and draw ends together so that yarn is doubled. Anchor on back of work at center of one side of medallion. Bring up through canvas. Twist needle five times; then slide it under satin stitches all the way around. Stop periodically and retwist yarn when necessary. It's far better to use twenty short strokes than to attempt to draw needle too far at one time. Twist only enough to get yarn under five or six strokes of satin stitch at a time; loosen up wherever possible, particularly under curved corner scallops.

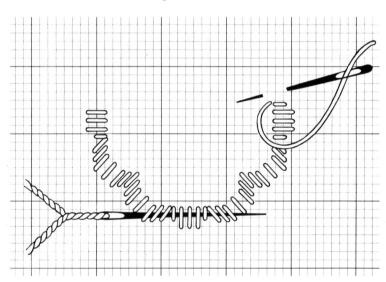

BACKSTITCH. This backstitch is worked over two mesh at a time, but only *after* basketweave is finished. Check graph for placement. Yarn should be slightly twisted—perhaps three or four times—just enough to distinguish backstitch from background basketweave.

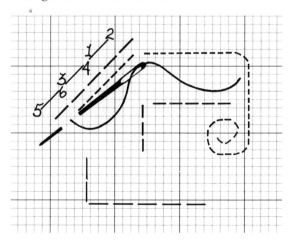

DOUBLE SERPENTINE STITCH. The serpentine stitch can be worked only *after* the backstitch has been finished. All serpentines should start from bottom of backstitch diagonals. Be sure to anchor the serpentine at the beginning and end of each side. The yarn should be twisted about ten times and retwisted when necessary. Draw yarn through each backstitch separately; this is not the place to save time. Keep loops even. For best effect begin and end at medallion edge. Don't attempt to carry yarn behind to next backstitch diagonal.

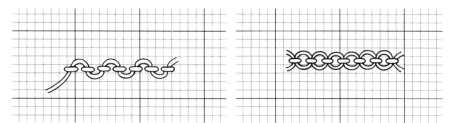

UPRIGHT CROSS-STITCH. Complete each upright cross-stitch before going on to the next. Be sure *all* top strokes go in same direction—in this instance, vertically.

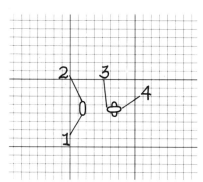

BASKETWEAVE STITCH (page 17). The last two rows are for use in finishing (see graph).

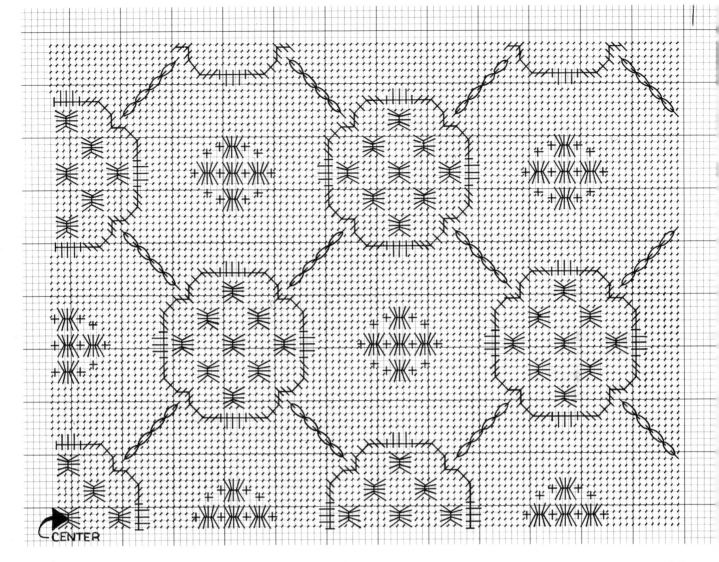

CENTER

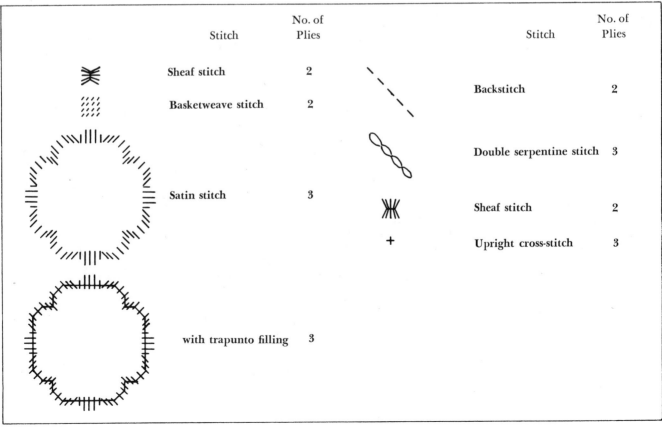

	Stitch	No. of Plies		Stitch	No. of Plies
✳	Sheaf stitch	2	– – – /	Backstitch	2
⫶⫶	Basketweave stitch	2	⬭⬭⬭	Double serpentine stitch	3
	Satin stitch	3	✳	Sheaf stitch	2
	with trapunto filling	3	+	Upright cross-stitch	3

Naked Blue

The finished project is shown in Plate 5.

Design area approximately 15 inches square (add margins)
#12 mono canvas
Yarn: #396 (lightest blue), 30 short (30-inch) strands Persian
   yarn; #395, 30 strands; #386, 50 strands; #385, 40
   strands; #334 (darkest blue), 90 strands

See *symbol guide* for stitch symbols, color guide, and number of plies of
yarn.

Special Note: Some of the stitches on this graph go beyond the center mark;
take them into account and proceed accordingly.

  This design is based on a four-way perspective utilizing both straight
and slanted stitches in five shades of one color. Work all four sections of
each stitch pattern before going on to the next; turn your canvas a quarter

turn for each section and proceed as in the first unless otherwise indicated.

The somewhat unorthodox use of canvas in this piece is based on my desire to use white as contrast; in this instance, I've used the bare (naked) white canvas threads to add to the three-dimensional quality in level as well as in color.

Keep checking graph for direction and placement of stitches. Keep straight stitches fairly loose but close to canvas; don't allow them to sag. On slanted stitches take similar care; don't distort canvas threads.

SATIN STITCH DIAMOND. Check graph for direction and placement.

FRENCH KNOT STITCH. These should be large and somewhat loose, since they're formed in single spaces and you don't want them to slide through when they're drawn together.

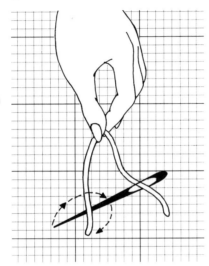

SATIN STITCH DIAMOND

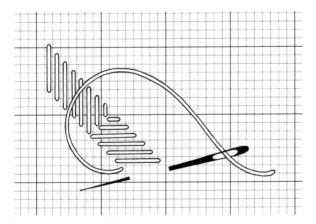

SATIN STITCH. Check graph for direction and placement.

BARE CANVAS. Shown on the graph as blank mesh—that is, background graph lines that show no stitch symbols.

CONTINENTAL STITCH (pages 15–16). Check graph for placement; keep tension even.

UPRIGHT DOUBLE CROSS-STITCH. Row *A*: Note direction of last stroke, in this instance from *upper left to lower right*. As you work in each new quarter section, change the order of your diagonal cross-strokes so that the top or final strokes *in this row* lie in the same direction on all four sides. Row *B*: Reverse the order of the strokes of the diagonal cross in this row so that the top stroke changes direction and slants from *lower left to upper right* in all four sections.

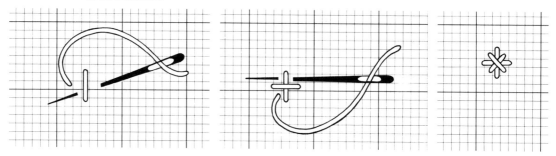

CONTINENTAL STITCH. Note on graph that there are two rows; check color guide.

BACKSTITCH. Check graph for placement; note space between stitches.

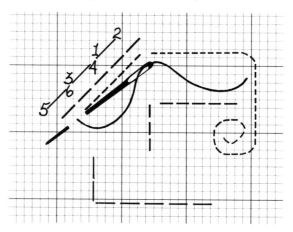

CONTINENTAL STITCH. Keep tension even.

BACKSTITCH. Check graph for placement; note space between stitches.

CONTINENTAL STITCH (two rows). One row skips every other mesh; check graph and color guide.

MOSAIC STITCH. Keep tension even.

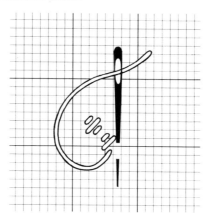

CONTINUOUS SCOTCH STITCH. Don't allow long strokes to sag.

MOSAIC STITCH. Keep tension even.

CONTINENTAL STITCH. Note on graph that there are two rows; check color guide.

CROSS-STITCH. Note on graph that one row is over every other mesh and the next row over each mesh; the top strokes lie in the same direction throughout.

CONTINENTAL STITCH. Check graph for placement; check color guide.

MOSAIC STITCH. Check tension.

CONTINUOUS SCOTCH STITCH. Don't allow long strokes to sag.

MOSAIC STITCH. Check tension.

CONTINENTAL STITCH. One row over every other mesh, next row over each mesh; check color guide.

BACKSTITCH. Check graph for placement; note space between stitches.

CONTINENTAL STITCH. Check graph for placement.

BACKSTITCH. Check graph for placement; note space between stitches.

CONTINENTAL STITCH. One row over every mesh; next row over every other mesh; check color guide.

UPRIGHT DOUBLE CROSS-STITCH. Row *C*: Note direction of last stroke, in this instance from *lower left to upper right*. Change the order of your diagonal cross-strokes in each new quarter section as necessary to make *all* top or final strokes in this row lie in the same direction. Row *D*: Reverse the order of strokes of the diagonal cross in this row so that the top stroke changes direction and slants from *upper left to lower right* throughout.

CONTINENTAL STITCH. Check graph for placement.

SATIN STITCH. Check graph for placement; see color guide.

BASKETWEAVE STITCH (page 17). The last two rows are for use by pillow maker, framer, or upholsterer for finishing (see graph, next page).

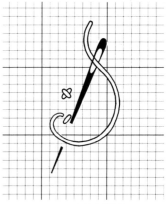

CROSS-STITCH

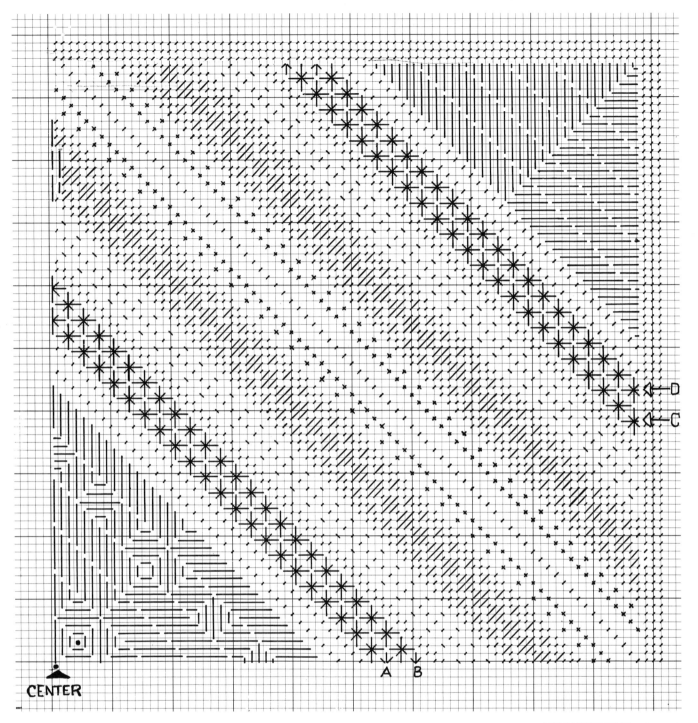

CENTER

A   B

D

C

See separate
chart for colors
for this project.

	Stitch	No. of Plies		Stitch	No. of Plies
‖‖‖	Satin stitch diamond	3		Backstitch	2
•	French knot stitch	3	⁄⁄	Mosaic stitch	2
‖‖‖	Satin stitch	3		Continuous Scotch stitch	2
⁄⁄	Continental stitch	2	×	Cross-stitch	2
✳	Upright double cross-stitch	3	⁄⁄⁄⁄	Basketweave stitch	2

Five shades, lightest to darkest: (1) #396, (2) #395,
(3) #386, (4) #385, (5) #334

Stitches	Color No.	Stitches	Color No.
Satin stitch diamond	4	Cross-stitch	5
French knot stitch (1)	2	Continental stitch	5
French knot stitch	5	Cross-stitch	5
Satin stitch diamond	1	Cross-stitch	5
Satin stitch	2	Continental stitch	5
Satin stitch	3	Continental stitch	4
Satin stitch diamond	4	Mosaic stitch	3
Satin stitch	5	Scotch stitch (continuous)	1
Continental stitch	5	Mosaic stitch	3
Continental stitch	5	Continental stitch	4
Upright double cross-stitch	3	Continental stitch	5
Upright double cross-stitch, reversed	4	Backstitch	3
Continental stitch	4	Continental stitch	5
Continental stitch	5	Backstitch	3
Backstitch	3	Continental stitch	5
Continental stitch	5	Continental stitch	4
Backstitch	4	Upright double cross-stitch	3
Continental stitch	5	Upright double cross-stitch, reversed	2
Continental stitch	4	Continental stitch	5
Mosaic stitch	3	Continental stitch	5
Scotch stitch (continuous)	1	Satin stitch	5
Mosaic stitch	3	Satin stitch	4
Continental stitch	4	Satin stitch	3
Continental stitch	5	Satin stitch	2
Cross-stitch	5	Satin stitch	1

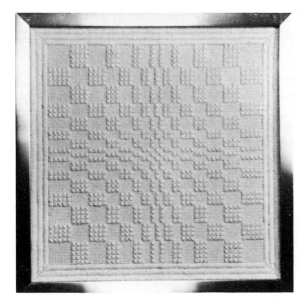
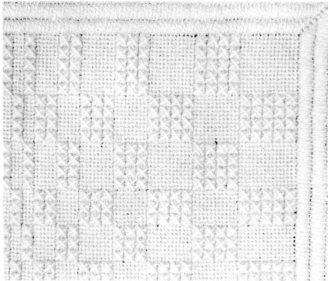

Optics

Design area approximately 15 inches square (add margins)
#12 mono canvas
Approximately 240 short (30-inch) strands Persian yarn
(color #010)

See *symbol guide* for stitch symbols and number of plies of yarn.

BASKETWEAVE STITCH (page 17). Since the basketweave stitch is generally worked from the top of an area downward, you may, at times, need to turn your canvas halfway around so the bottom edge becomes the temporary top edge of your canvas. When you've finished this part of the design, turn the canvas back to its original position and proceed. Work 3 or 4 inches into design, then do reverse Scotch stitch. Go back to basketweave and proceed once more.

REVERSE SCOTCH STITCH. Check graph for direction of stitches.

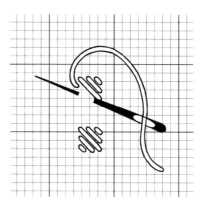

DIAGONAL CROSS-STITCH TIE-DOWN. This stitch is worked over completed reverse Scotch stitches; it requires yarn to be twisted at least ten times for crisp effect and retwisted whenever necessary. Wait until there's a respectable number of finished Scotch stitch groups, then work diagonal cross-stitches in rows to tie down. Be sure top strokes *all* slant in the same direction, in this case from *lower left* to *upper right*.

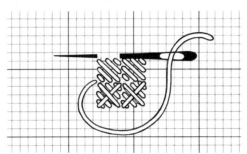

UPRIGHT GOBELIN STITCH. This stitch is four threads high, so the strokes frequently have a tendency to be too loose. Be watchful and keep the strokes close to the canvas without distorting the canvas threads. Check graph for change in direction.

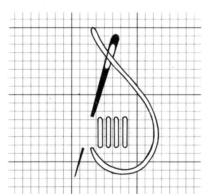

BACKSTITCH. This backstitch is made diagonally over a single mesh at a time. Work with light tension in order to avoid distorting canvas threads.

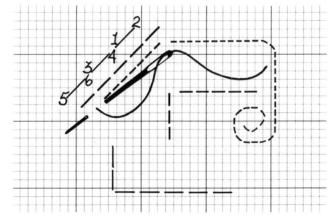

BASKETWEAVE STITCH (page 17). The last two rows are for use by pillow maker, framer, or upholsterer for finishing (see graph, next page).

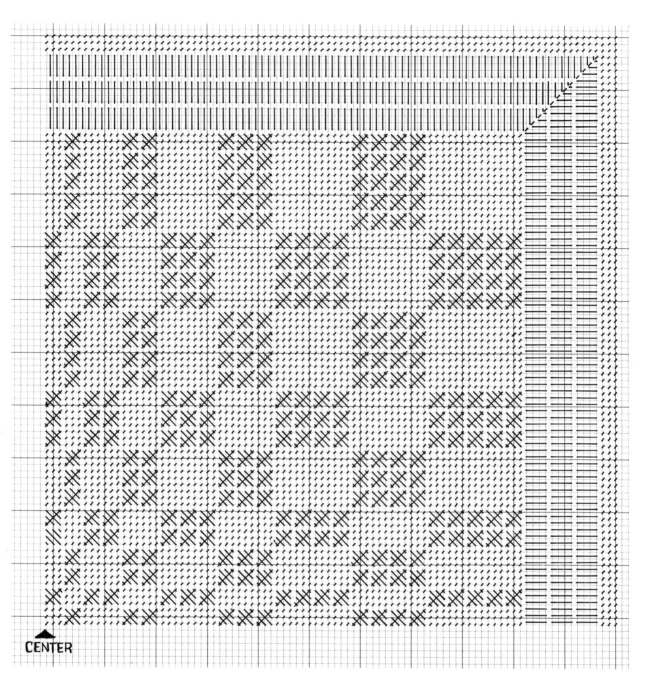

CENTER

	Stitch	No. of Plies
⫶⫶⫶	Basketweave stitch	2
⫻⫻	Reverse Scotch stitch	2
✕	Diagonal cross-stitch tie-down	2
||||	Upright Gobelin stitch	3
⁃⁃⁃	Backstitch	2

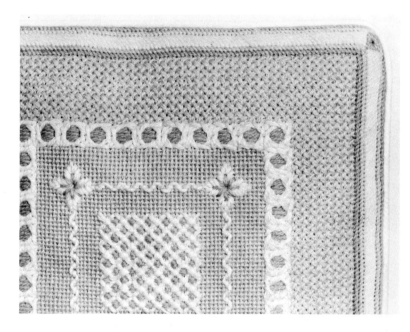

Orange Sherbet

The finished project is shown in Plate 6.

Design area approximately 10 inches square (add margins)
#12 mono canvas
130 short (30-inch) strands Persian yarn: #005 white, 75;
#988 light orange, 40; #978 dark orange, 15
See *symbol guide* for stitch symbols, colors, and number of plies of yarn.

Special Note: Some of the stitches on this graph go beyond the center mark; take them into account and proceed accordingly.

LATTICE STITCH. Work upward to the left and downward to the right in diagonal rows.

UPRIGHT CROSS-STITCH TIE-DOWN. Work stitches upward to the left and downward to the right in diagonal rows. Complete each stitch before going on to the next, keeping *all* top strokes going in the same direction. For added interest, you might consider doing this tied-down upright cross-stitch with a *vertical* top stroke and the following upright cross-stitch with a *horizontal* top stroke.

UPRIGHT CROSS-STITCH. Complete each upright cross-stitch before going on to the next; work stitches upward to the left and downward to the right in diagonal rows. Be sure *all* top strokes go in same direction.

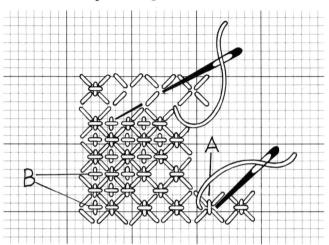

BASKETWEAVE STITCH (page 17). Since the basketweave stitch is generally worked from the top of an area downward, you may, at times, need to turn your canvas halfway around so the bottom edge becomes the temporary top edge of your canvas. When you've finished this part of the design, turn the canvas back to its original position and proceed.

TIP-OF-LEAF STITCH. Work strokes from outside in toward the center. Check graph for placement; turn your canvas as necessary.

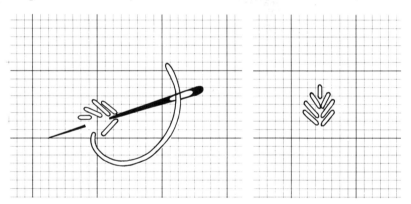

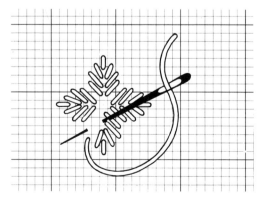

STAR STITCH. This stitch is worked on top of finished tip-of-leaf. Check graph for placement.

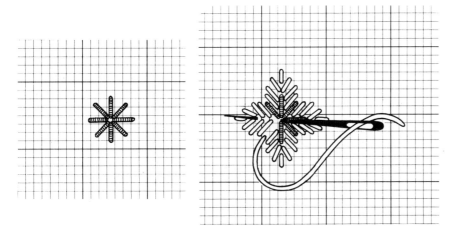

BACKSTITCH. This backstitch is worked over two canvas threads (not mesh) at a time, but only *after* basketweave is finished. Check graph for placement.

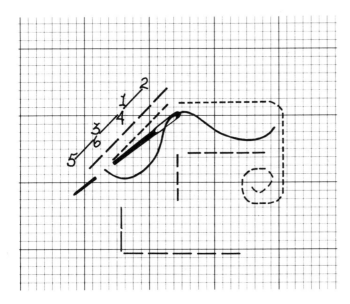

SINGLE SERPENTINE STITCH. The serpentine stitch can be worked only *after* the backstitch has been finished and it's best executed when only one whole side of the design is done at a time. Be sure to anchor the serpentine at the beginning and end of each side; don't attempt to go around corners. The yarn should be twisted about ten times and retwisted when necessary. For best effect, draw yarn through each backstitch separately. Keep loops even.

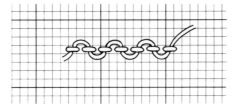

SATIN STITCH. Check graph for placement. This stitch should be completed before proceeding with square Shisha stitch. Keep stitch full but not sagging; if necessary use an additional ply of yarn.

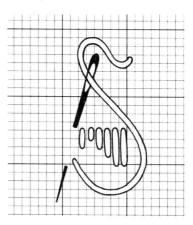

SQUARE SHISHA STITCH. You've probably seen this used in fastening tiny mirrors to Indian embroideries; here it's used to frame the satin stitch center, which should be done first for best effect.

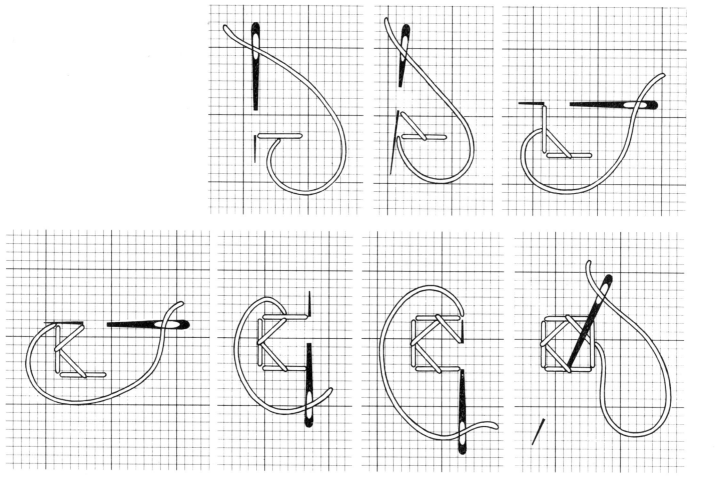

WOVEN PLAIT STITCH. Make a special effort to keep tension even throughout.

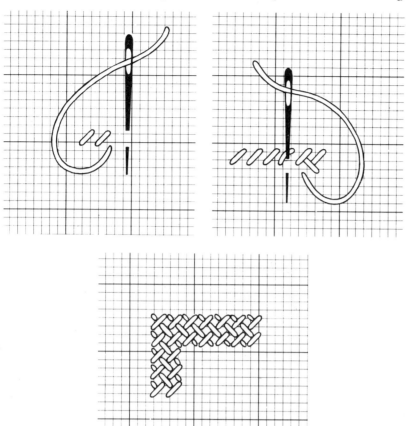

OUTLINE STITCH. In this instance, finish the woven plait stitch and the slanted Gobelin stitch first. Note that outline stitch goes *forward over* two mesh, then *back under* one. Check *symbol guide* for color changes and the graph for placement.

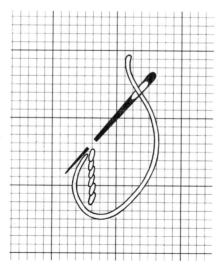

SLANTED (OBLIQUE) GOBELIN STITCH. This stitch is four threads high and four threads wide, so the strokes are somewhat lengthy and frequently have a tendency to be too loose. Be watchful and keep the strokes close to the canvas without distorting the canvas threads. Your yarn will kink up from time to time; drop your needle and let the yarn unwind itself. Complete the entire row before working the outline stitches on either side.

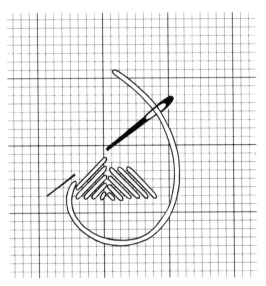

ALGERIAN SQUARE EYELET. Use a single Algerian square eyelet in each corner of project, working it at each end of the slanted Gobelin stitch band; check graph for placement. These should be finished before rows of outline stitch are worked.

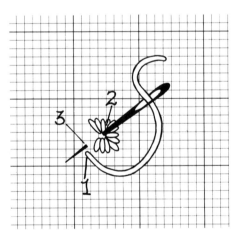

OUTLINE STITCH. These rows should be done only *after* slanted Gobelin, Algerian square eyelet, and basketweave stitches have been completed.

BASKETWEAVE STITCH (page 17). These two rows are for use by pillow maker, framer, or upholsterer for finishing (see graph).

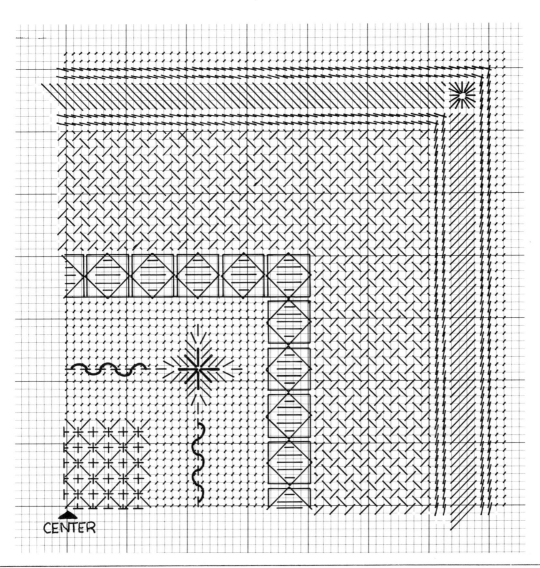

CENTER

	Stitch	Color	No. of Plies		Stitch	Color	No. of Plies
	Lattice stitch	white #005	2		Square Shisha stitch	white #005	2
+	Upright cross-stitch A	white #005	3		Satin stitch	dark orange #978	3
	Upright cross-stitch B	dark orange #978	3		Woven plait stitch	light orange #988	2
	Basketweave stitch	light orange #988	2		Outline stitch	dark orange #978	2
	Tip-of-leaf stitch	white #005	2			light orange #988	
	Star stitch	dark orange #978	2		Algerian square eyelet	dark orange #978	2
– – – –	Backstitch	white #005	2		Slanted (oblique) Gobelin stitch	white #005	2
～	Single serpentine stitch	white #005	2				

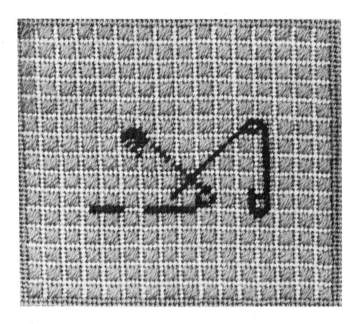

Pincushion for Baby

The finished project is shown in **Plate 2**.

Design area approximately 5½ inches square (add margins)
#12 mono canvas
All short (30-inch) strands Persian yarn: #731 blue, 2 strands;
#852 dark coral, 18 strands; #853 light coral, 12 strands
See *symbol guide* for stitch symbols, colors, and number of plies of yarn.

CONTINENTAL STITCH (pages 15–16). To start, find circled center stitch on graph. Work part of light coral network and then do safety pins; go back and fill in with Scotch stitches.

SCOTCH STITCH. Be a little firm in working the long center stitch; it has a tendency to sag. Don't distort the canvas threads; just be sure the long stitch lies close to the canvas.

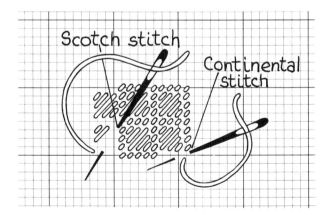

BASKETWEAVE STITCH (page 17). These two rows are for use in finishing (see graph).

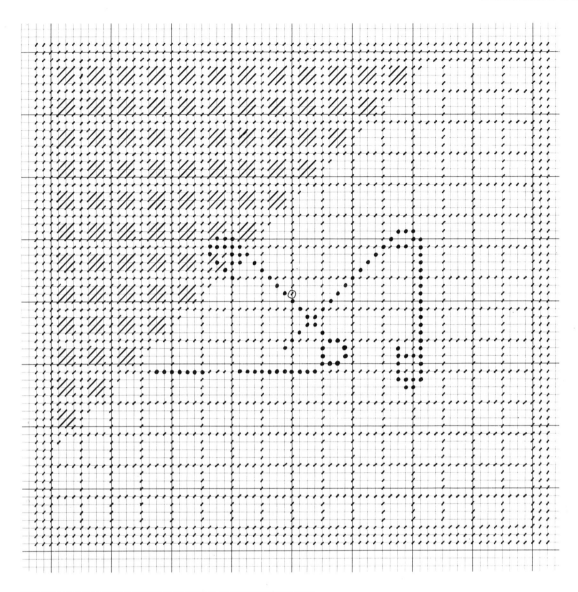

	Stitch	Color	No. of Plies
·······	Continental stitch	blue #731	2
⁄⁄⁄	Scotch stitch	dark coral #852	2
⁝	Continental stitch	light coral #853	2

 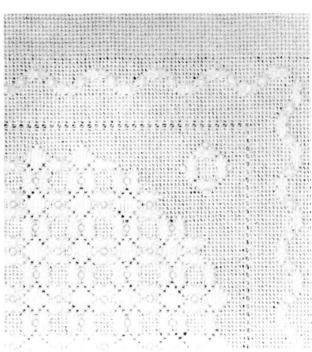

Potpourri

Design area approximately 15 inches square (add margins)
#12 mono canvas
Approximately 5 ounces short (30-inch) strands Persian yarn
(color #010)

See *symbol guide* for stitch symbols and number of plies of yarn.

Special Note: Some of the stitches on this graph go beyond the center mark; take them into account and proceed accordingly.

SATIN STITCH DIAMOND. Keep stitches fairly loose but close to canvas; don't allow them to sag.

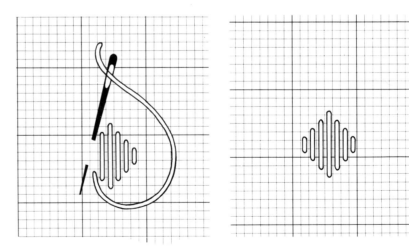

SHEAF STITCH. Watch your tension; let the five strokes of each stitch just lie on the canvas. Check graph for direction and placement.

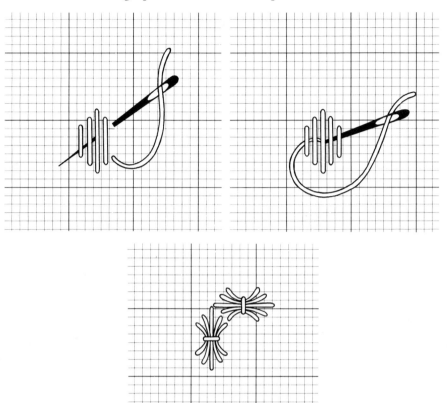

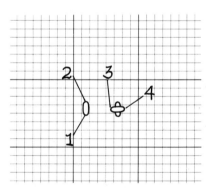

UPRIGHT CROSS-STITCH. Complete each upright cross-stitch before going on to the next; *all* top strokes should be horizontal.

BASKETWEAVE STITCH (page 17). Since the basketweave stitch is generally worked from the top of an area downward, you may, at times, need to turn your canvas halfway around so the bottom edge becomes the temporary top edge of your canvas. When you've finished this part of the design, turn the canvas back to its original position and proceed. Check *symbol guide* for number of plies.

SHEAF STITCH. See above.

UPRIGHT DOUBLE CROSS-STITCH. Follow the same order of strokes throughout, checking the graph for placement. Work an upright cross over four canvas threads, then a diagonal cross over two, finishing each upright double cross-stitch before going on to the next. Note direction of last stroke and be sure *all* top strokes lie the same way.

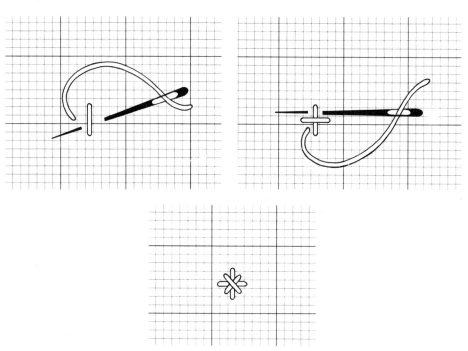

BASKETWEAVE STITCH (page 17). Check plies.

HEMSTITCH. This stitch is worked from right to left and is formed by reaching *back over* two canvas threads and *forward under* four, pulling tightly on yarn to draw the two threads together, thus leaving space between stitches. When you've pulled your yarn tightly, hold it down on canvas with your free thumb while you form next stitch; this helps keep stitch tension even.

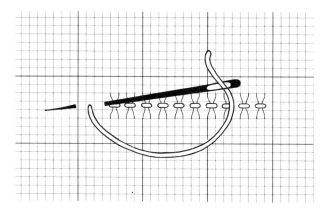

BASKETWEAVE STITCH (page 17). The last two rows are for use by pillow maker, framer, or upholsterer for finishing (see graph).

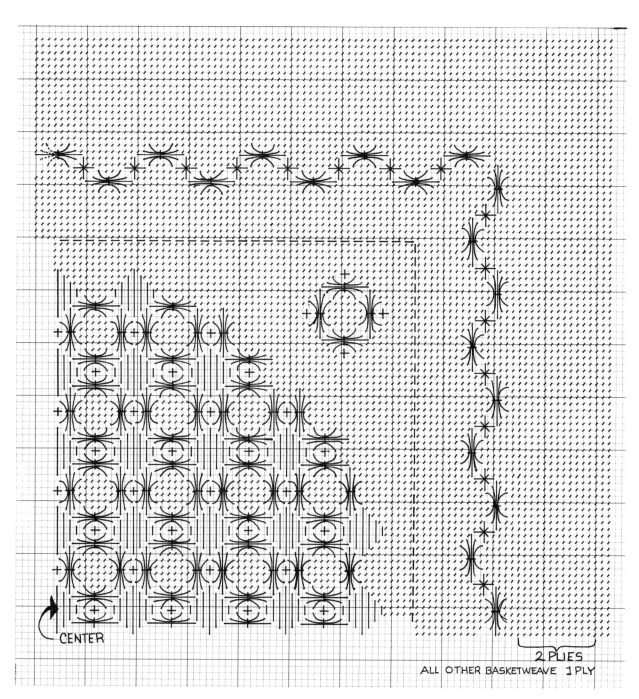

CENTER

2 PLIES
ALL OTHER BASKETWEAVE 1 PLY

	Stitch	No. of Plies		Stitch	No. of Plies
∥∣∥∣∥	Satin stitch diamond	3	⁄⁄⁄⁄	Basketweave stitch	1, 2
✳	Sheaf stitch	3	✳	Upright double cross-stitch	3
+	Upright cross-stitch	3	− − −	Hemstitch	2

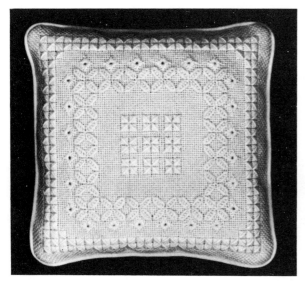

Quadrille

Design area approximately 10½ inches square (add margins)
#12 mono canvas
130 short (30-inch) stands Persian yarn (color #010)
See *symbol guide* for stitch symbols and number of plies of yarn.

SCOTCH STITCH, REVERSED. The long middle stroke is apt to sag a little unless you draw it a trifle more closely; don't distort canvas threads. Keep checking graph for direction changes.

TIE-DOWN STITCH. Twist strand five times. Retwist as necessary.

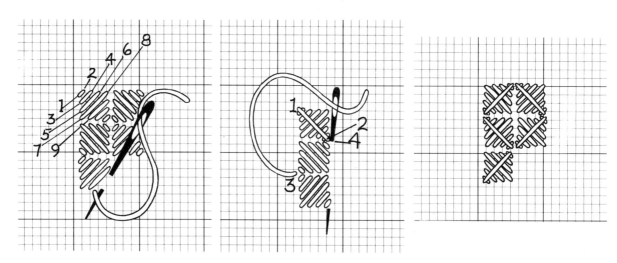

BASKETWEAVE STITCH (page 17). Since the basketweave stitch is generally worked from the top of an area downward, you may, at times, need to turn your canvas halfway around so the bottom edge becomes the temporary top edge of your canvas. When you've finished this part of the design, turn the canvas back to its original position and proceed.

DIAGONAL FLY STITCH. Check graph for changes in direction. Diagonal fly stitch is always worked from "tip of leaf" downward toward "stem." Turn canvas so top edge becomes bottom edge to make first diagonal fly stitch leaf. Turn back to make second leaf.

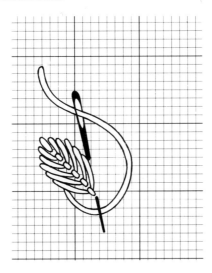

ALGERIAN DIAMOND EYELET. To form eyelet properly, tension of yarn must be controlled. When making stitches on each side, *between* points, pull firmly; release tension on yarn to make corner or point stitches. Keep eyelet centers uniform in size.

SCOTCH STITCH, REVERSED AND TIED DOWN. Keep checking graph for changes in direction.

"TRUE" BASKETWEAVE STITCH. Note that in forming each stitch, the needle ducks diagonally behind one mesh to move into proper position for the next stitch.

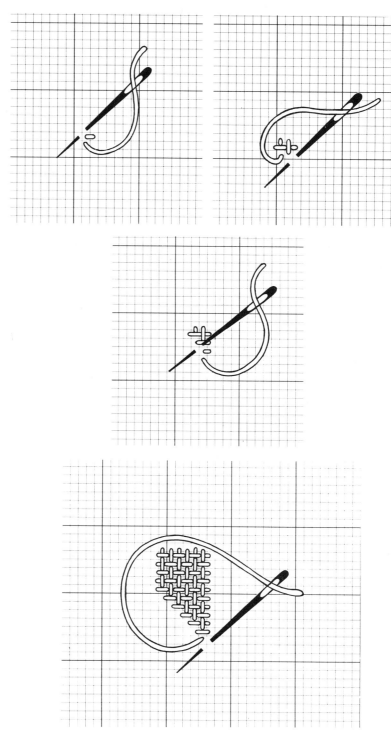

BASKETWEAVE STITCH (page 17). These two rows are for use by pillow maker, framer, or upholsterer for finishing (see graph).

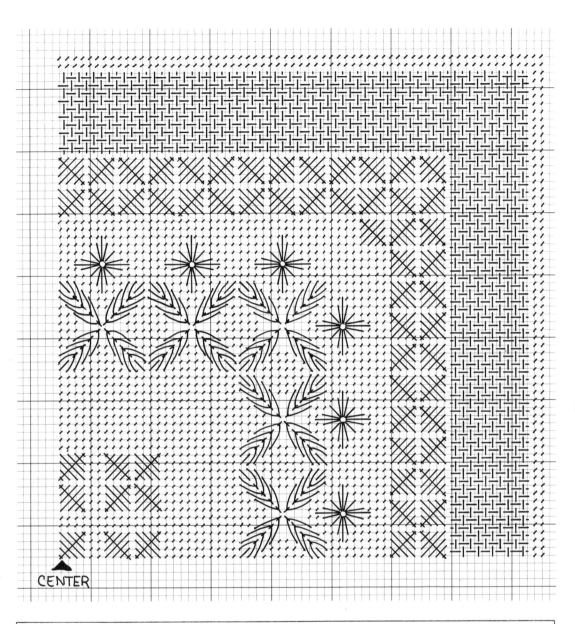

CENTER

	Stitch	No. of Plies		Stitch	No. of Plies
	Scotch stitch, reversed and tied down	2		Algerian diamond eyelet	2
	Basketweave stitch	2		"True" basketweave stitch	2
	Diagonal fly stitch	2			

Queen Anne

Design area approximately 10 inches square (add margins)
#12 mono canvas
120 short (30-inch) strands Persian yarn (color #010)
See *symbol guide* for stitch symbols and number of plies of yarn.

DIAGONAL FLY STITCH. Diagonal fly stitch is always worked from "tip of leaf" downward toward "stem." Turn canvas so top edge becomes bottom edge to make first diagonal fly stitch leaf. Turn back to make second leaf. Check graph for directional changes.

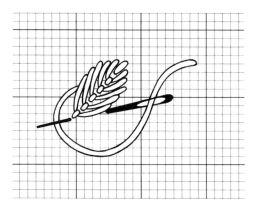

BASKETWEAVE STITCH (page 17). Since the basketweave stitch is generally worked from the top of an area downward, you may, at times, need to turn your canvas halfway around so the bottom edge becomes the temporary top edge of your canvas. When you've finished this part of the design, turn the canvas back to its original position and proceed.

SMYRNA CROSS-STITCH, REVERSED AND TIED DOWN. Follow same sequence of construction throughout project, that is, an upright cross first, then a diagonal cross, and finish with tied-down backstitch strokes in clockwise direction. Check graph for placement.

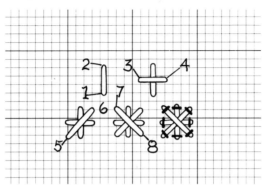

SATIN STITCH A. Note variations of sections *A* and *B* on graph and follow pattern carefully.

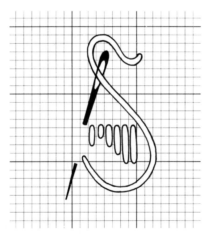

SATIN STITCH B. Check graph for pattern.

UPRIGHT GOBELIN STITCH. Keep tension even; don't distort canvas threads.

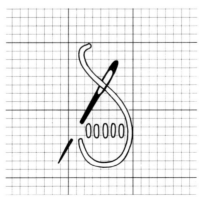

SMYRNA CROSS-STITCH, REVERSED. Be sure *all* top strokes slant from *upper left* to *lower right*, throughout the project.

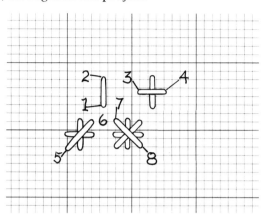

UPRIGHT GOBELIN STITCH. See graph.

SCOTCH STITCH, REVERSED. Check graph for changes in direction of stitches.

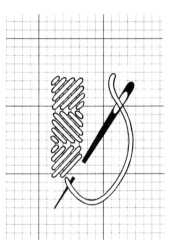

UPRIGHT GOBELIN STITCH. See graph.

SMYRNA CROSS-STITCH, REVERSED. See graph.

SMYRNA CROSS-STITCH, REVERSED AND TIED DOWN. Work one as motif in each corner of band; check graph for placement.

UPRIGHT GOBELIN STITCH. See graph.

BASKETWEAVE STITCH (page 17). Last two rows are for use by pillow maker, framer, or upholsterer for finishing (see graph).

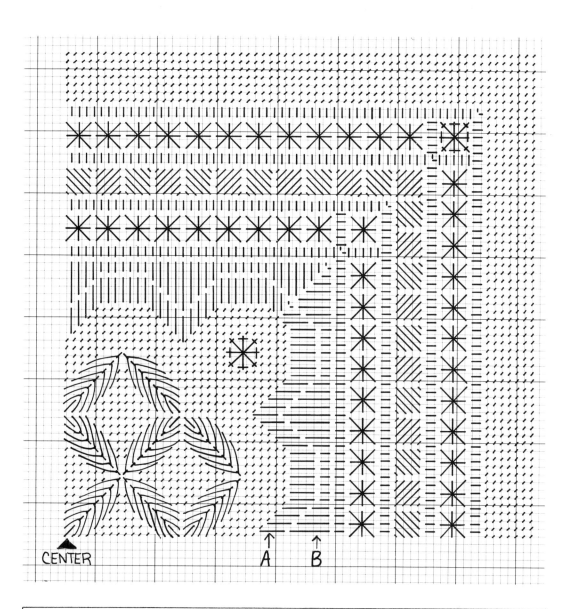

CENTER

A B

Stitch	No. of Plies		Stitch	No. of Plies
Diagonal fly stitch	2		Upright Gobelin stitch	3
Basketweave stitch	2		Smyrna cross-stitch, reversed	2
Smyrna cross-stitch, reversed and tied down	2		Scotch stitch, reversed	2
Satin stitch	3			

Red Mirror Frame

The finished project is shown in **Plate 1**.

Design area: length of sides optional; width of design band
approximately 3½ inches (add margins)
#10 mono canvas
The design area of illustrated frame (Plate 1) required 4½
ounces #R50 (red), 11 30-inch strands #R10 (dark red), and 30
strands #496 (beige)
See *symbol guide* for stitch symbols, colors, and number of plies of yarn.

First decide on size of finished and framed piece; this will be measurement of outer edge of design band. Add 4 inches in width (2-inch margin for each side) and 4 inches in depth (2-inch margin for each side). This measurement is for cutting your canvas; the center will remain blank and unworked and will back up the mirror that will later be mounted inside your worked design band.

When you've determined the size you want, mark canvas with inner and outer margins, allowing 36 mesh between them for your work. Start at upper right-hand corner of design area and proceed with basketweave stitch.

BASKETWEAVE STITCH (page 17). Since the basketweave stitch is generally worked from the top of an area downward, you may, at times, need to turn your canvas halfway around so the bottom edge becomes the temporary top edge of your canvas. When you've finished this part of the design, turn the canvas back to its original position and proceed.

SMYRNA CROSS-STITCH. Follow the same sequence of construction throughout the project; that is, the diagonal cross first, then an upright cross. Finish with the horizontal stroke on top as your last stroke before proceeding to the next Smyrna cross-stitch.

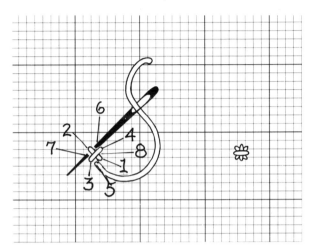

BACKSTITCH. There are two rows of backstitches; check graph for placement. These *must* wait for Smyrna cross and basketweave stitches to be completed. Each backstitch is worked over a single canvas thread.

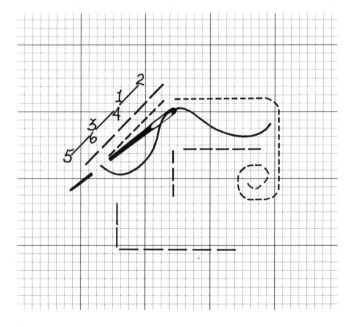

STARFLOWER STITCH #3. Check graph for placement; follow carefully.

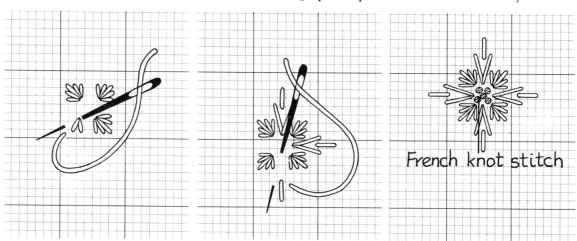

French knot stitch

FRENCH KNOT STITCH. Make the four French knots over mesh; leave the central one for last. Make the central French knot a trifle looser than the others.

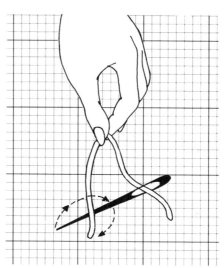

BAR WITH DIAGONAL CROSS-STITCH. Use same order throughout; first lay down horizontal stroke (bar) over four canvas threads, then stitch diagonal cross over two canvas threads, *always* keeping top stroke lying in same direction. Check graph for placement and changes in direction.

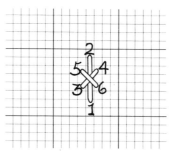

BASKETWEAVE STITCH (page 17). See graph; fill in around starflowers wherever canvas is exposed, even if not on graph.

SCOTCH STITCH, REVERSED AND TIED DOWN. The long middle stroke is apt to sag a little unless you draw it a trifle more closely; don't distort canvas threads. Keep checking graph for direction changes. For tie-down, twist strand five times. Retwist as necessary.

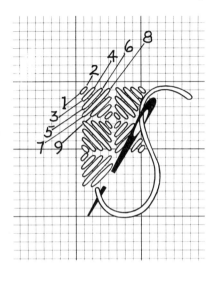

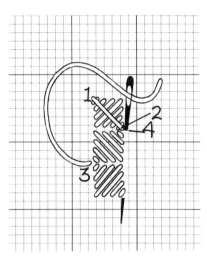

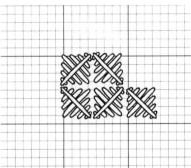

BASKETWEAVE STITCH (page 17). See graph, next page.

BACKSTITCH. There are two rows of backstitches; check graph for placement. These *must* wait for tied-down Scotch stitches and basketweave to be completed. Each backstitch is worked over a single canvas thread.

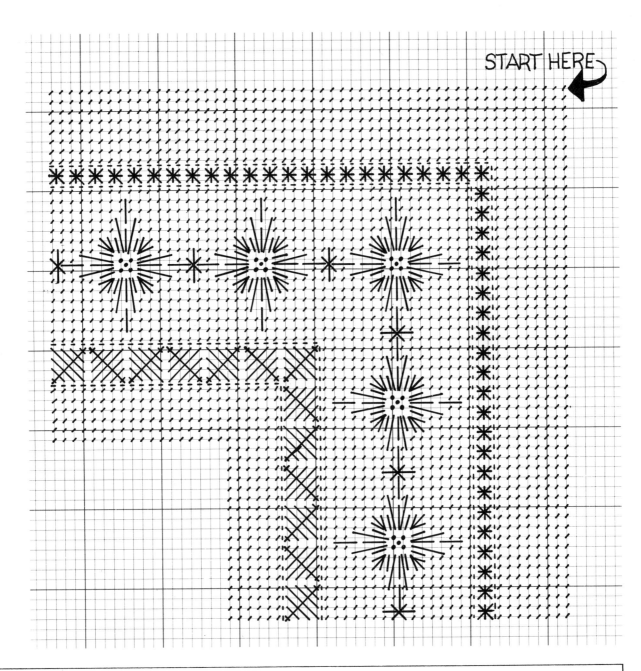

	Stitch	Color	No. of Plies		Stitch	Color	No. of Plies
	Basketweave stitch	red #R50	3	•	French knot stitch	red #R50	3
✳	Smyrna cross-stitch	red #R50	3	⋇	Bar with diagonal cross-stitch	beige #496	3
-----	Backstitch	dark red #R10	2	⬛⬛	Scotch stitch, reversed and tied down	red #R50	3
✸	Starflower stitch #3	beige #496	3				

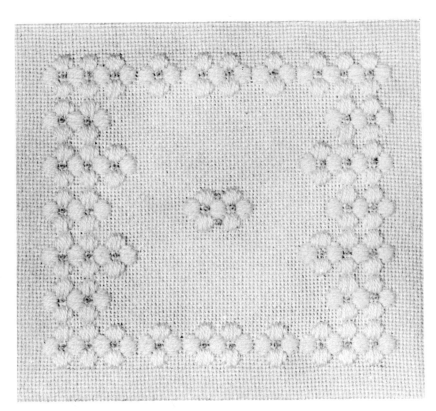

Ring Bearer's Pillow

The finished project is shown in Plate 7.

This little ring bearer's pillow can be a lot of things to a lot of people. Primarily it's intended to circumvent youthful inattention and to anchor the elusive wedding ring so that it's in view right up to the moment when it needs to be produced; the narrow blue velvet ribbons do that job handsomely.

Sometimes the best man carries the ring pillow, and gratefully; it gives him something reasonable to do with his hands, and he need never fumble through four or five pockets when the magical moment comes!

But that's still pretty limited use, unless you've made it as a wedding gift (in which case you might add the lucky couple's initials and the big date). However, it can be romantic (even sentimental) and pragmatic.

It can become a kind of instant heirloom and supply the traditional "something old, something new, something borrowed, something blue" if your assorted children, godchildren, nieces, nephews, friends' and neighbors' offspring, even your grandchildren, use and enjoy it as each of them marries.

It could also be a lovely way to make a generous and self-perpetuating gift to your house of worship; a pillow, specially made by you for the purpose, could then be loaned for use by other members of the congregation, in return for which they would be expected to make a contribution.

> Design area approximately 9 inches × 8 inches (add margins)
> #12 mono canvas
> 120 strands (30-inch) Persian yarn (color #010); 6 strands #758 blue (for French knots)
> Cord: 12 (continuous) yards Persian yarn (color #010)
> Tassels: 4 30-inch strands Persian yarn (color #010); approximately 28 (continuous) yards Persian yarn (color #010)
> Ribbon: 24 inches of light blue velvet, ⅜ inch wide

See *symbol guide* for stitch symbols, colors, and number of plies of yarn.

SATIN FLOWER PETAL STITCH. Work a trifle loosely so that petals are full; don't let strokes sag.

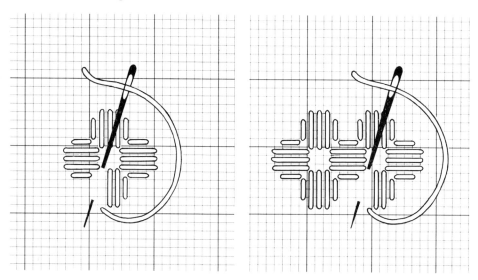

BASKETWEAVE STITCH A (page 17). Since the basketweave stitch is generally worked from the top of an area downward, you may, at times, need to turn your canvas halfway around so the bottom edge becomes the temporary top edge of your canvas. When you've finished this part of the design, turn the canvas back to its original position and proceed. Use one ply throughout central area. Keep tension even.

FRENCH KNOT STITCH. Check *symbol guide* for color and plies. Work a *little* loosely or knot will disappear when drawn together.

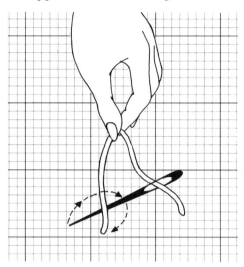

SATIN FLOWER PETAL STITCH. See opposite. Placement here is somewhat tricky; check graph and follow carefully.

BASKETWEAVE STITCH B. At this point switch to 2-ply and limit 2-ply basketweave to area *outside* all satin flower petals. Those few places between and in centers of petal stitches should be done in single ply. Last two rows are for use by pillow maker in finishing.

TWISTED CORD (requires two people). Fold a 12-yard strand of yarn in four; make an overhand knot at each end. Each person slips a pencil into loop at one end and, holding yarn loosely just below the pencil with one hand, twists the pencil with the other hand. *Extremely important*: both persons twist pencils clockwise, holding the yarn absolutely taut until it begins to kink; catch center over a doorknob or hook. Then bring pencils together for one person to hold, while the other transfers one end loop, leaving both loops on one pencil. Remove twisted yarn from doorknob and hold twist at center. Sliding one hand down yarn toward this end and releasing it at short intervals, let yarn twist by itself. Secure each knot separately by winding sewing thread where twist stops. Fasten off with a few knotted stitches. Trim ends off evenly.

TASSELS. Make four twisted cords using the technique above and one 30-inch strand of yarn for each. For each tassel cut 40 6-inch strands. Fold the twisted cord in half; place center of tassel pieces across doubled cord near loop end. Draw cord ends over tassel strands and through loop; pull tightly. Holding all tassel ends together, wrap a piece of yarn three or four times around the whole bunch, about 1 inch from folded end of tassel; knot securely. Trim tassel ends.

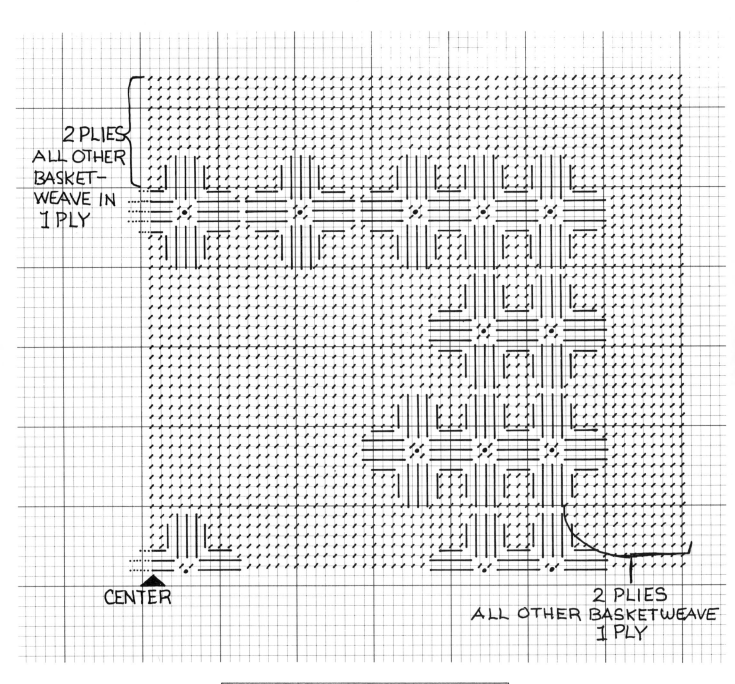

2 PLIES
ALL OTHER
BASKET-
WEAVE IN
1 PLY

CENTER

2 PLIES
ALL OTHER BASKETWEAVE
1 PLY

	Stitch	Color	No. of Plies
	Basketweave stitch A	#010	1
	Basketweave stitch B	#010	2
	Satin flower petal stitch	#010	3
•	French knot stitch	blue #758	3

Round Web Pincushion

The finished project is shown in Plate 2.

Design area approximately 5 inches square (add margins)
#5 French Penelope canvas
Pat-Rug yarn: #550, 10 long (60-inch) strands
Persian yarn: #545, 9 short (30-inch) strands; #565, 25 short (30-inch) strands

See *symbol guide* for stitch symbols, colors, and number of plies of yarn.

WEB STITCH, WRAPPED. Using rug yarn fastened securely to canvas, place spokes from outside to center of web. Then, using fresh strand of securely anchored rug yarn, proceed to wrap spokes. Make three rows of wrapping, going *back over* one spoke and *forward under* two, and so on.

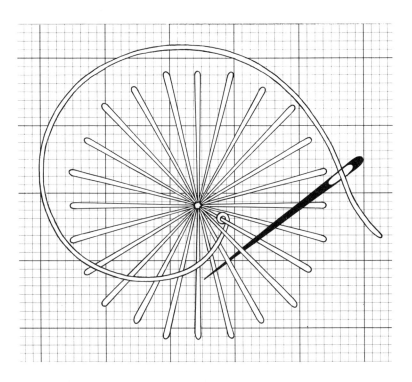

ROSETTE STITCH. Change direction and proceed to make two full rows of rosette stitch going *forward over* two spokes and *back under* one. Do not pull too tightly; don't shift the spokes as you wrap them.

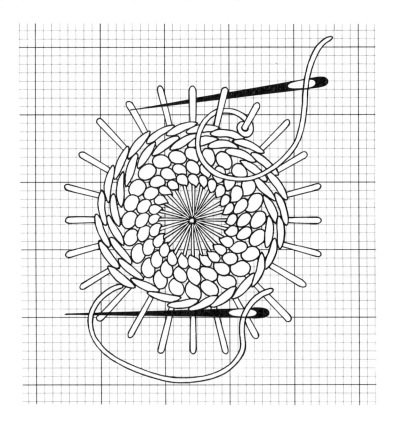

WEB STITCH, WRAPPED. See opposite. It is not necessary to start a fresh strand for wrapping; just continue with strand you've been using until it needs replacement. This section of web requires three rows of wrapping.

BASKETWEAVE STITCH (page 17). Since the basketweave stitch is generally worked from the top of an area downward, you may, at times, need to turn your canvas halfway around so the bottom edge becomes the temporary top edge of your canvas. When you've finished this part of the design, turn the canvas back to its original position and proceed. Separate canvas threads so that you can stitch over single mesh (ten to the inch instead of five), and follow graph for placement, using Persian yarn. Fill in exposed canvas between spokes of web even if not shown on graph.

SMYRNA CROSS-STITCH, REVERSED. Using Persian yarn (check *symbol guide* for color and plies), make upright cross first, then top with diagonal cross, completing each Smyrna before going on to the next stitch. Be sure *all* top strokes match.

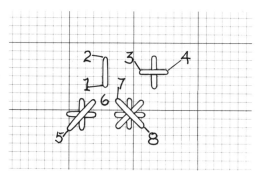

BASKETWEAVE STITCH (page 17). The last two rows are for use in finishing (see graph, next page).

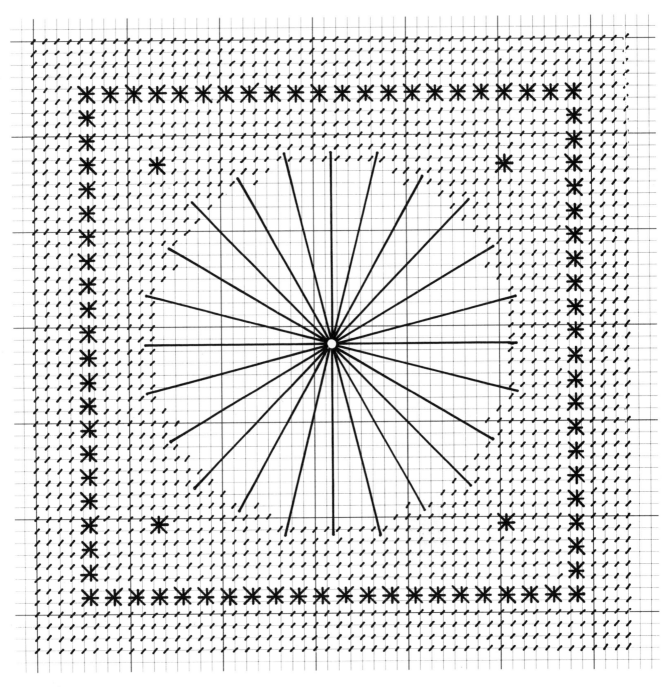

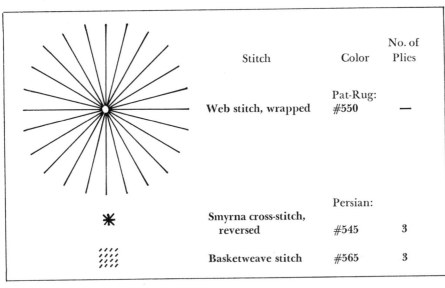

Stitch	Color	No. of Plies
	Pat-Rug:	
Web stitch, wrapped	#550	—
	Persian:	
Smyrna cross-stitch, reversed	#545	3
Basketweave stitch	#565	3

Square Web Pincushion

The finished project is shown in Plate 2.

Design area approximately 5 inches square (add margins)
#5 French Penelope canvas
Pat-Rug yarn: #738, 6 long (60-inch) strands
Persian yarn: #738, 28 short (30-inch) strands; #748, 8 short
(30-inch) strands

See *symbol guide* for stitch symbols, colors, and number of plies of yarn.

WEB STITCH, WRAPPED. Anchor rug yarn firmly for base strokes at beginning
and end of web. Start to wrap with fresh long strand after anchoring it

securely. It will take at least eight rows of wrapping, with some extra wrapping at corners, going *back over* one spoke and *forward under* two, and so on.

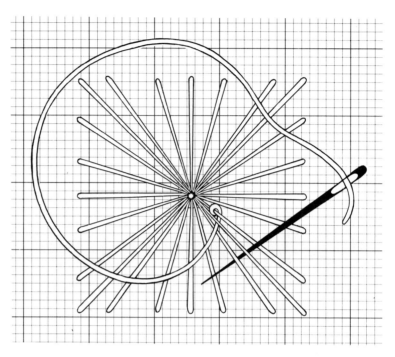

BASKETWEAVE STITCH (page 17). Since the basketweave stitch is generally worked from the top of an area downward, you may, at times, need to turn your canvas halfway around so the bottom edge becomes the temporary top edge of your canvas. When you've finished this part of the design, turn the canvas back to its original position and proceed. Separate canvas threads so that you can stitch over single mesh (ten to the inch instead of five); follow graph for placement, using Persian yarn. Fill in exposed canvas between spokes of web even if not shown on graph.

SMYRNA CROSS-STITCH, REVERSED. Using Persian yarn, make the upright cross first, then top with diagonal cross, completing each Smyrna before going on to the next stitch. Be sure *all* top strokes match.

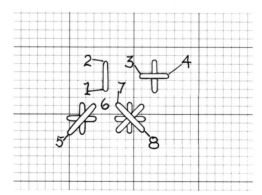

BASKETWEAVE STITCH (page 17). The last two rows are for use in finishing (see graph).

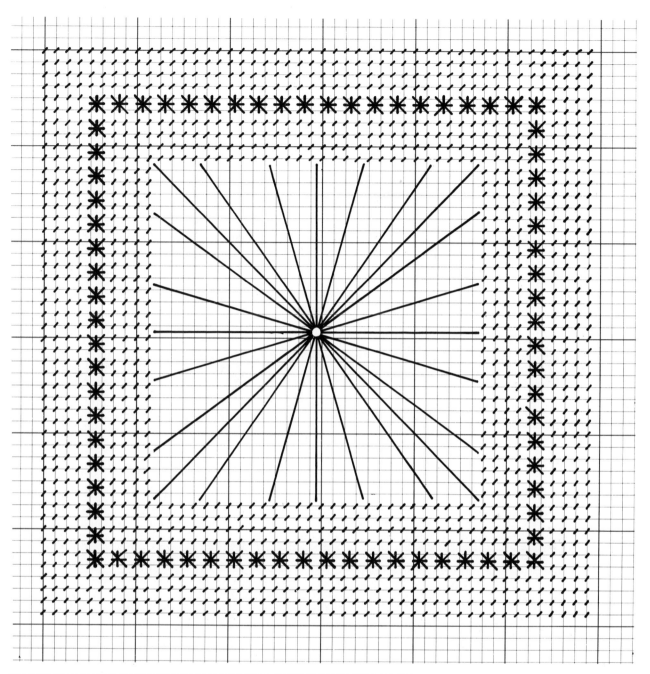

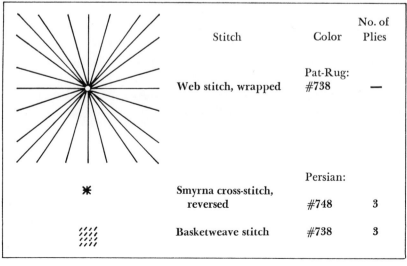

Stitch	Color	No. of Plies
Web stitch, wrapped	Pat-Rug: #738	—
Smyrna cross-stitch, reversed	Persian: #748	3
Basketweave stitch	#738	3

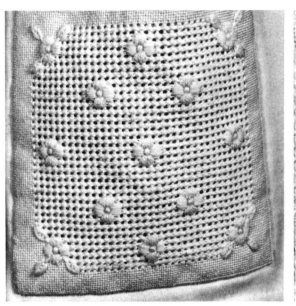
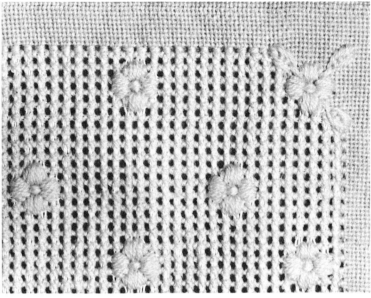

Stole Pocket

Design area 10 inches square (add margins)
#12 mono canvas
110 short (30-inch) strands Persian yarn (color #010)
See *symbol guide* for stitch symbols and number of plies of yarn.

Special Note: Some of the stitches on this graph go beyond the center mark; take them into account and proceed accordingly.

SATIN FLOWER PETAL STITCH. Work somewhat loosely so petals are full, but don't allow strokes to sag. Keep tension even. Check graph for placement and direction.

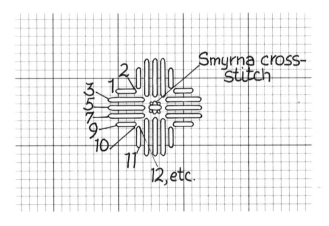

SMYRNA CROSS-STITCH. Follow the same order throughout, first doing a diagonal cross, then an upright cross, with *every* final or top stroke a horizontal one.

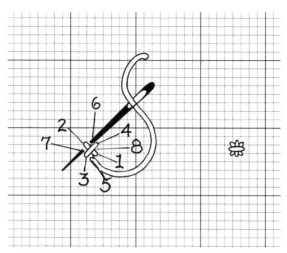

DIAGONAL FLY STITCH. Check graph for changes in direction. Diagonal fly stitch is always worked from "tip of leaf" downward toward "stem"; turn your canvas as necessary.

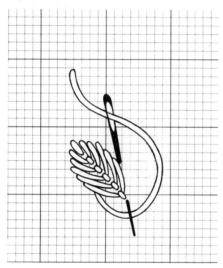

Note: The satin flower petal stitches, the Smyrna cross-stitches, and the diagonal fly stitches must *all* be completed before you go on to the next stitch.

DOUBLE PULLED CROSS-STITCH. As each stroke is laid diagonally across three mesh (see graph), pull the yarn gently but firmly and hold it down with your free thumb while you make the next stroke. Keep your tension even to ensure that the open spaces are uniform throughout.

First work each row *horizontally to the right*, making only one-half of a cross-stitch all the way; return *horizontally to the left*, adding the second halves of the cross-stitches. Finish all the horizontal rows of completed single pulled cross-stitches in the design area before going on. To complete double pulled cross-stitches, work vertical rows in same manner, first *from bottom to top*, then returning *from top to bottom*.

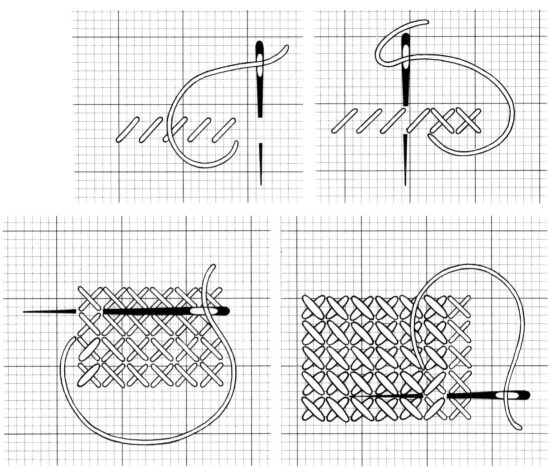

BASKETWEAVE STITCH (page 17). See graph. This stitch must be completed before you do backstitch. Check graph and note that the last two rows change direction.

BACKSTITCH. This backstitch reaches back over three canvas threads and, instead of the needle carrying the yarn directly forward behind six threads to make the next stitch, the needle should first be passed through the back of the nearest basketweave stitches, bypassing the open spaces so the long back stroke doesn't show through them.

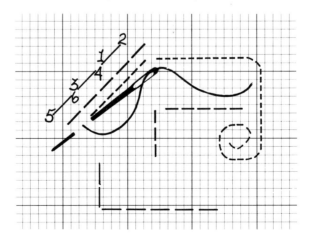

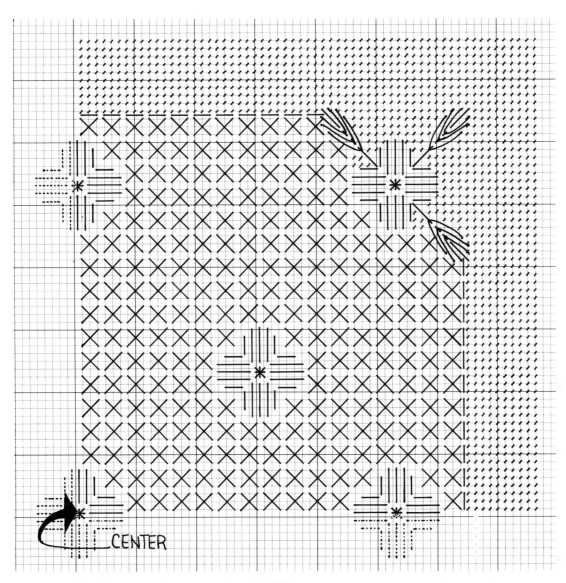

CENTER

	Stitch	No. of Plies
	Satin flower petal stitch	3
✳	Smyrna cross-stitch	2
✕	Double pulled cross-stitch	3
	Diagonal fly stitch	2
– – –	Backstitch	3
	Basketweave stitch	2

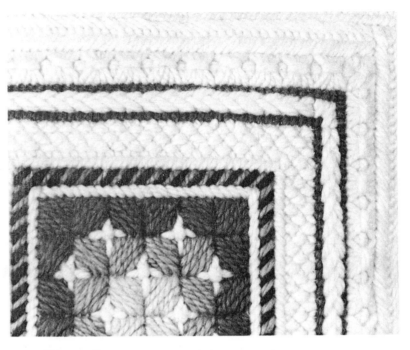

Texas Star

The finished project is shown in Plate 8.

Design area approximately 15 inches square (add margins)
#5 French Penelope canvas
Yarn: short (30-inch) strands Pat-Rug yarn: #909, 4 strands;
#919, 15 strands; #929, 5 strands; #939, 1 strand; #010, 5 ounces
See *symbol guide* for stitch symbols and colors.

Special Note: Some of the stitches on this graph go beyond the center mark; take them into account and proceed accordingly.

SCOTCH STITCH, REVERSED. Check graph for changes in direction of stitch. Keep tension light, without allowing stitches to sag.

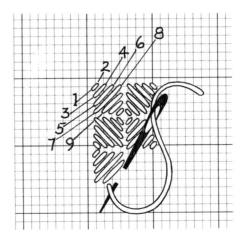

KNOTTED UPRIGHT CROSS-STITCH. Scotch stitch, reversed, *must* be finished before this stitch is worked. Observe stitch guide carefully and make all strokes in the same order throughout. Check graph for placement.

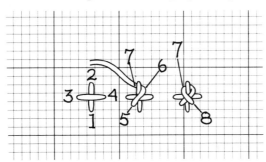

OUTLINE STITCH. Keep tension even and check graph for direction. Do not distort canvas threads.

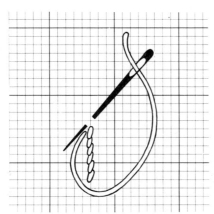

SLANTED (OBLIQUE) GOBELIN STITCH. This stitch is four threads high and four threads wide, so the strokes are somewhat lengthy and tend to be somewhat loose. Be watchful and keep the strokes close to the canvas without distorting the canvas threads. Your yarn will kink up from time to time; drop your needle and let the yarn unwind itself.

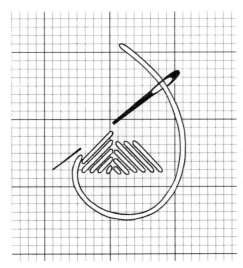

OUTLINE STITCH, REVERSED. Check graph for direction and placement.

UPRIGHT CROSS-STITCH. Complete each upright cross-stitch before going on to the next; this stitch is best worked in diagonal rows upward to the left and downward to the right. *All* top strokes of stitches should be horizontal.

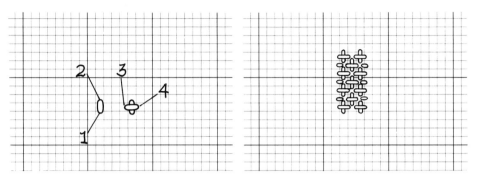

CONTINENTAL STITCH (pages 15–16). Check graph for placement and direction.

ENCROACHING CROSS-STITCH. See graph for small compensation stitches at beginning and end of each row. Do not allow stitches to sag.

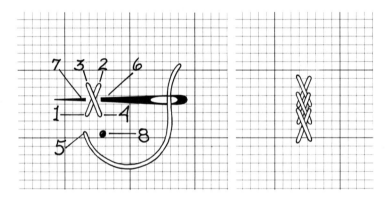

SATIN STITCH CORNER. In each of the four instances where this stitch occurs, all strokes slant toward center of canvas.

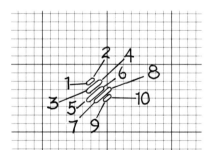

CONTINENTAL STITCH, REVERSED. Check graph for placement and direction.

SHEAF STITCH. Watch your tension; let the five strokes of each stitch just lie on the canvas. The tie-down stroke, when drawn into place, should cover two threads of canvas. Check graph and note that outer strokes of each sheaf share spaces with those of following sheaves.

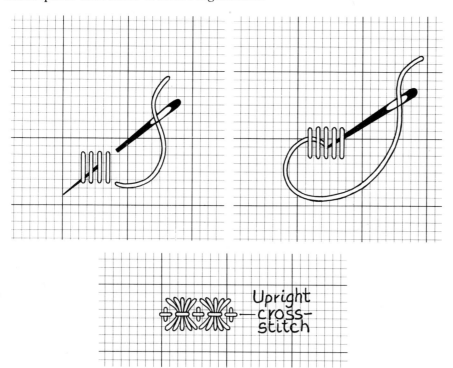

CORNER SHEAF STITCH. Check graph for stroke placement. Don't allow long center stroke to sag. Be sure this stitch is in place before attempting mosaic stitch.

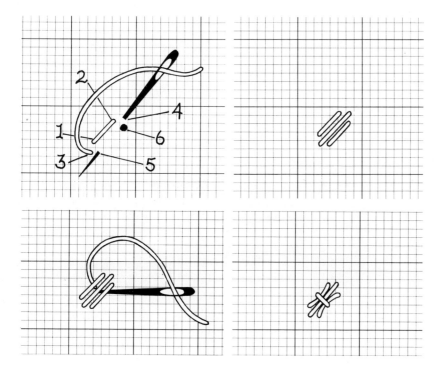

MOSAIC STITCH. Check graph for placement.

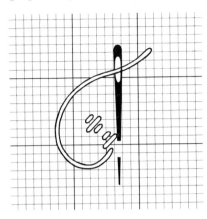

FLY STITCH. Fly stitch *must* be worked from the top downward. Check graph for direction and placement of compensation stitches.

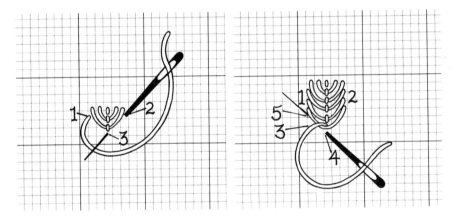

OUTLINE STITCH, REVERSED. Check graph for direction and placement.

SMYRNA CROSS-STITCH, REVERSED. Follow same sequence of construction throughout project, that is, an upright cross first, then a diagonal cross. Finish with the diagonal stroke from upper left to lower right on top, as your last stroke; then proceed to the next stitch.

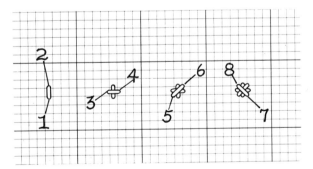

OUTLINE STITCH. Check graph for direction and placement.

BASKETWEAVE STITCH (page 17). These two rows are for use by pillow maker, framer, or upholsterer for finishing (see graph).

CENTER

Stitch	Color	Stitch	Color
Scotch stitch, reversed (inner four)	1	Encroaching cross-stitch	#010
Scotch stitch, reversed (second row)	2	Satin stitch corner	#010
Scotch stitch, reversed (outer row)	3	Sheaf stitch	#010
Knotted upright cross-stitch	#010	Corner sheaf stitch	#010
Outline stitch	#010	Mosaic stitch	#010
Slanted (oblique) Gobelin stitch	2 and 4 alternately	Fly stitch	#010
Upright cross-stitch	#010	Smyrna cross-stitch, reversed	#010
Continental stitch, reverse continental stitch	4	Basketweave stitch	#010

Pat-Rug yarn, therefore no list of plies needed.

Four shades of green, lightest to darkest:
(1) #909, (2) #919, (3) #929, (4) #939

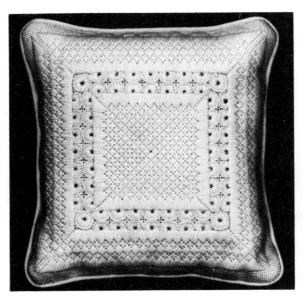
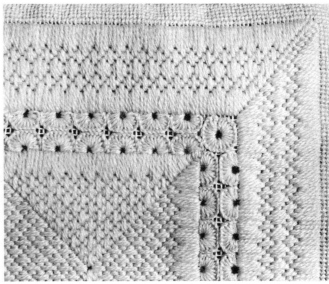

Turn of the Century

Design area approximately 11 inches square (add margins)
#12 mono canvas
150 short (30-inch) strands Persian yarn (color #010)
See *symbol guide* for stitch symbols, colors, and number of plies of yarn.

HUNGARIAN STITCH. Note four-way treatment on graph. Be sure to keep tension relaxed and even throughout.

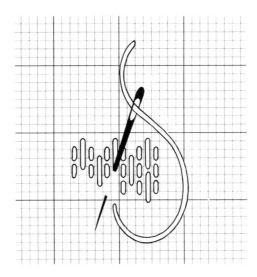

SATIN STITCH A. Note variance in sections *A*, *B*, *C*, and *D* on graph. Keep checking graph for directional changes. Keep stitches fairly loose but close to canvas; don't allow them to sag.

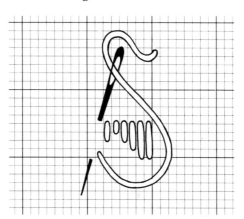

BUTTONHOLE, HALF-ROUND. Note that here the naked canvas is essential to the design. Draw yarn gently but firmly to form stitches; try not to distort canvas threads. Keep centers of stitches uniform in size.

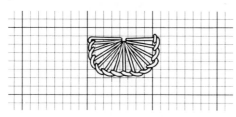

BUTTONHOLE, ROUND. There's one in each corner of the band of half-round buttonhole stitches, and they're done with the same relaxed but controlled tension.

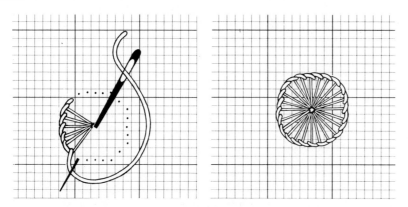

SATIN STITCH B. See section *B* on graph; follow pattern carefully.

HUNGARIAN STITCH. Check graph for placement.

SATIN STITCH DIAMOND (C). See section *C* on graph; follow pattern carefully.

HUNGARIAN STITCH. Check graph for placement.

SATIN STITCH D. See section *D* on graph; follow pattern carefully.

BASKETWEAVE STITCH (page 17). The last two rows are for use by pillow maker, framer, or upholsterer for finishing (see graph, next page).

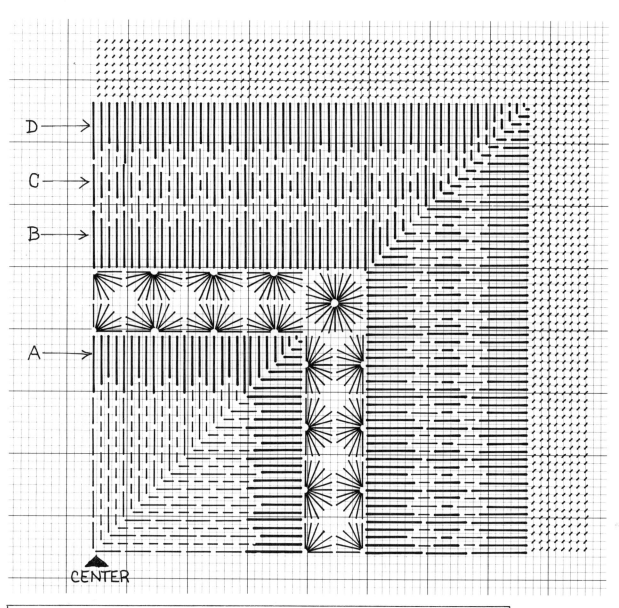

D →

C →

B →

A →

CENTER

	Stitch	No. of Plies		Stitch	No. of Plies
∣ ∣∣ ∣	Hungarian stitch	3	☀	Buttonhole stitch, round	2
‖‖‖‖‖	Satin stitch	3	∣∣∣∣∣	Satin stitch diamond	3
⛭	Buttonhole stitch, half-round	2	⫶⫶⫶	Basketweave stitch	2

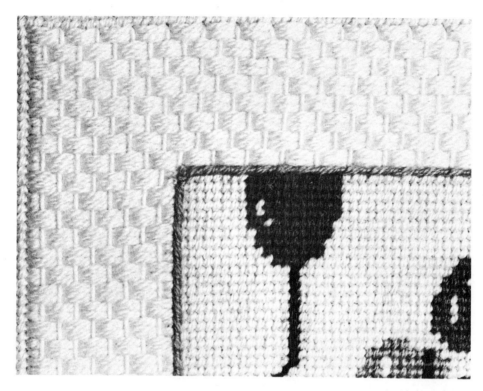

Up, Up, and Away!

The finished project is shown in Plate 9.

Design area approximately 10½ inches × 11 inches (add margins)
#10 mono canvas
All 30-inch strands Persian yarn: #G37 seafoam, 47; #Y44 yellow, 9; #579 green, 8; #733 blue, 7; #R50 red, 6; #050 black, 6; #968 orange, 5; #748 aqua, 3; #005 off-white, 3

See *symbol guide* for stitch symbols, colors, and number of plies of yarn.

BASKETWEAVE STITCH (page 17). Since the basketweave stitch is generally worked from the top of an area downward, you may, at times, need to turn your canvas halfway around so the bottom edge becomes the temporary top edge of your canvas. When you've finished this part of the design, turn the canvas back to its original position and proceed.

CONTINENTAL STITCH (pages 15–16). Use this stitch for all balloon strings and for off-white highlights on balloons. Watch out for any increase in tension; keep your continental stitches at the same level as the basketweave stitches.

WILLOW STITCH. This stitch is worked in two parts: the first is, in effect, a double brick stitch (shown in stitch guide); the second part consists of long strokes of tightly twisted yarn woven under the double brick stitches (not through canvas) and firmly anchored at each end of stroke.

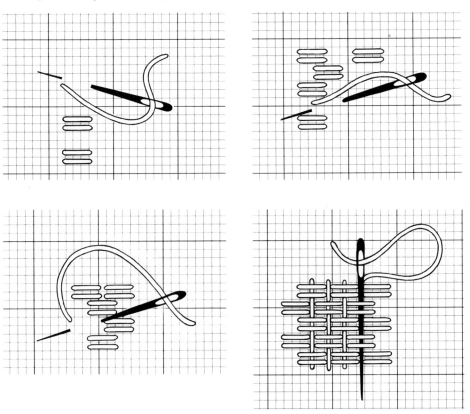

OUTLINE STITCH. This stitch reaches *forward over* three mesh (not canvas threads) and *back under* one. Basketweave design section and willow stitch must be completed before outline stitch.

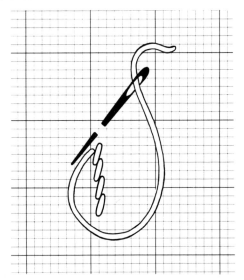

BASKETWEAVE STITCH (page 17). These two rows are for use in finishing by the framer or pillow maker (see graph).

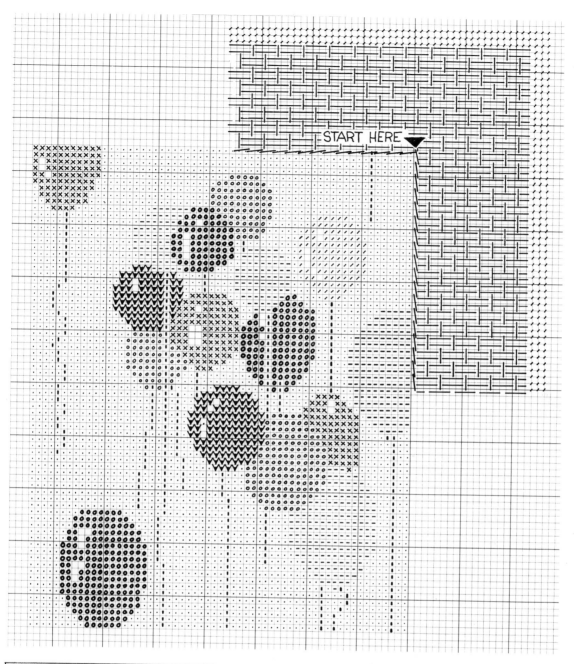

START HERE

Stitch	Color	No. of Plies		Stitch	Color	No. of Plies
• Basketweave stitch	seafoam #G37 (background)	3	°	Basketweave stitch	orange #968	3
– Basketweave stitch	yellow #Y44	3	'	Basketweave stitch	aqua #748	3
ᵥ Basketweave stitch	green #579	3	□	Continental stitch	off-white #005	
• Basketweave stitch	blue #733	3		Willow stitch	white #001	3
× Basketweave stitch	red #R50	3				
' Continental stitch	black #050	3		Outline stitch	green #579	3

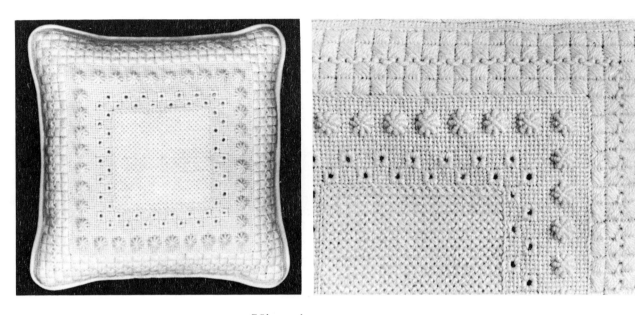

Victoriana

Design area approximately 10½ inches square (add margins)
#12 mono canvas
160 short (30-inch) strands Persian yarn (color #010)
See *symbol guide* for stitch symbols and number of plies of yarn.

Special Note: Some of the stitches on this graph go beyond the center mark; take them into account and proceed accordingly.

WOVEN PLAIT STITCH. Make a special effort to keep tension even throughout.

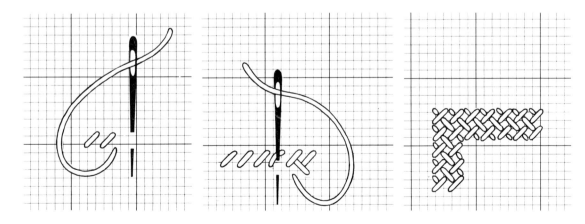

OUTLINE STITCH. Outline stitch is generally worked after the stitches on either side of it are finished. In this instance, finish the woven plait and the Algerian square eyelet stitches first. Note that the stitch goes *forward over* two canvas threads, *not* mesh, then *back under* one.

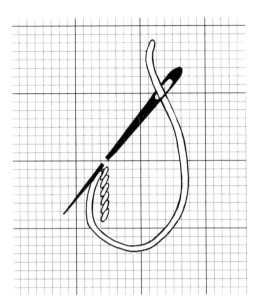

ALGERIAN SQUARE EYELET. To keep outer edges of stitch square, pull yarn gently but firmly toward you when working stitches on sides, more loosely when working corner stitches. Keep eyelet centers uniform in size.

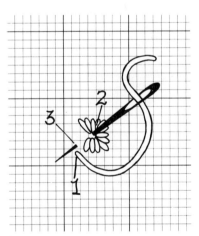

BASKETWEAVE STITCH (page 17). Since the basketweave stitch is generally worked from the top of an area downward, you may, at times, need to turn your canvas halfway around so the bottom edge becomes the temporary top edge of your canvas. When you've finished this part of the design, turn the canvas back to its original position and proceed.

TINY WRAPPED WEB. Keep tension even and firm when placing base strokes. There are three rows of wrapping: be firm at center of web, slightly looser as you work the second row and as you approach the outer edges. Try to make all the wrapped webs as uniform as possible in size and shape; they're an important aspect of the finished piece.

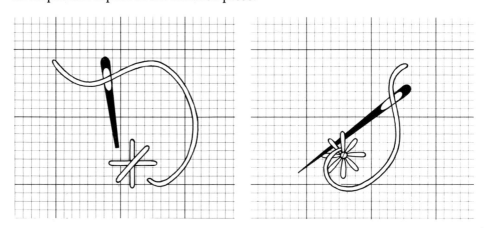

OUTLINE STITCH. In this instance, finish the basketweave and Scotch stitch, reversed, *first*. Note that this stitch goes *forward over* two canvas threads, *not* mesh, then *back under* one.

SCOTCH STITCH, REVERSED. Be a little firm in working the long center stitch; it has a tendency to sag a bit. Don't distort the canvas threads; just be sure the long stitch lies close to the canvas.

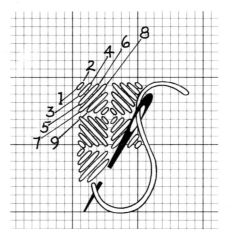

BACKSTITCH. This backstitch is worked over two canvas threads, *not* mesh, at a time, but only *after* Scotch stitch, reversed, is finished.

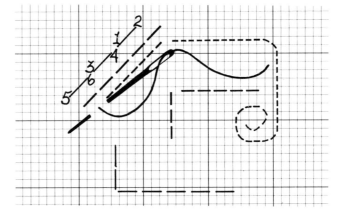

SINGLE SERPENTINE STITCH. The serpentine stitch can be worked only *after* the backstitch has been completed and is best executed when only one whole side of the design is done at a time. Be sure to anchor the serpentine at the beginning and end of each side; don't attempt to go around corners. The yarn should be twisted about ten times and retwisted when necessary; keep loops even. For best effect, draw yarn through each backstitch separately.

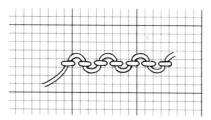

OUTLINE STITCH. In this instance, finish the Scotch stitch, reversed, and basketweave *first*. Note that this stitch goes *forward over* two canvas threads, *not* mesh, then *back under* one.

BASKETWEAVE STITCH (page 17). The last two rows are for use by pillow maker, framer, or upholsterer for finishing (see graph, next page).

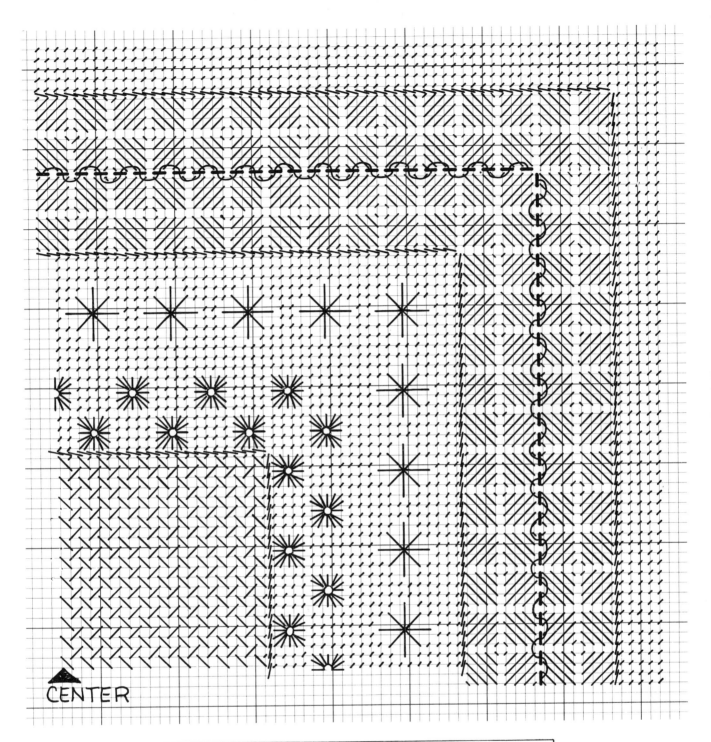

CENTER

	Stitch	No. of Plies		Stitch	No. of Plies
	Woven plait stitch	2		Tiny wrapped web	2
	Algerian square eyelet	2		Scotch stitch, reversed	2
	Basketweave stitch	2		Backstitch	2
	Outline stitch	2		Single serpentine stitch	2

The
Notebook

When I first began to play with stitchery as a sculptural concept, I found myself constantly having to make small interruptive moves to try out stitches in different ways before I could proceed with my design idea. I needed to know how many threads of canvas would be required by each stitch; whether it could be made higher, lower, wider, narrower; how it could be used as a specimen or ornamental stitch if I needed it as an accent; and so on. This was frustrating and time consuming, and I found it a maddening challenge. The result was the Notebook (see Plate 10).

The notebook itself is a substantial hardcover loose-leaf notebook with three large (2-inch) rings. It has thirty loose-leaf sheets of five-to-the-inch graph paper and thirty acetate sleeves, each encasing a black sheet. When I have made a sample stitch, I white-glue a 1/4-inch-wide line about 1/2 inch away from the stitch. When the glue dries I cut the canvas just inside the outer edge of the glue line, brush the *whole* back of the stitched canvas with white glue, and press it in place on one of the graph sheets. I draw a simplified stitch guide on the graph paper next to the sample stitch. Any pertinent information also goes on the same sheet, particularly if there's room for diversity with the stitch. The number of plies used, the canvas gauge, the color numbers, the names of the yarns used, any special handling required or "tricks" used in the sample stitch—all these can be of enormous help long after you've forgotten what you've done.

The combination of a stitch guide for how-to, a finished sample so you can judge its characteristics, information you need to know or be reminded of, and blessed relief from the need to interrupt your progress in order to experiment is a marvelous boon I strongly urge you to try. The loose-leaf arrangement itself is worth its weight in gold because you can take any pages you want out of the binder, lay them all on the floor or dining room table, and shuffle them around while you decide.

125

When you're finished, you can put the sheets back in any order you like—you can add or substitute or experiment further. You can put pages temporarily in the order you plan to use for a particular piece, or when you have enough pages you can sort them by category or three-dimensional qualities.

Above and beyond all of this, of course, you're compiling a sampler that's truly beyond appraisal. Not only will you have all the stitches you've learned and forgotten, but you'll have stitch guides to jog your memory of how to go about making those stitches.

Designing Sculptured Needlepoint Stitchery

By now you've probably sensed that there are as many ways to design sculptured needlepoint stitchery as there are enthusiasts willing to explore its potentials. I hope you'll be one of those enthusiasts.

The important thing, of course, is to keep that third dimension in mind at all times. To do that successfully, you'll need to know what a stitch looks like when it's done. Will it be flat and therefore reflect lots of light and look silky? Will it be flat but patterned and break up in light refraction? Will it be slightly raised and ropy? Or braided? Or smoothly rounded? Will it be individually shaped? And if it is, will it be round? Square? A diamond shape? Could it be oval if it needed to be? What about stripes or ridges, polka-dots or hobnails?

Every time you experiment with a stitch, cut out the variations that appeal to you, paste them on a notebook page, quickly jot down everything you need to know about making the stitch, and go back to your work in progress.

The next time you decide to do some sculptured needlepoint stitchery, you can leaf through your notebook and, comparing the varying heights and other characteristics of your stitches, you will undoubtedly find that a lot of your preliminary work in designing has already been done and a lot of your questions have been answered.

Naturally the stitches in these pages are by no means the limit of what you can use in sculptured needlepoint stitchery, but merely the limit of what one book of designs could cover. The projects in this book are meant to give you a wide range of design styles and to demonstrate how versatile sculptured needlepoint stitchery can be. I suggest you do several of them to get the feel of what it's all about. Then examine them all over again and think about the different elements that compose each of those you like. Try to visualize those components used together. Practice a few stitches in rows or in blocks. Play with them. Put them together in any way that occurs to you.

Try different gauges of canvas, different weights of yarn: 1-, 2-, or 3-ply Persian, shag, or rug yarn. Try stitches at different angles. As the friendly old lady said when asked by a stranger how one gets to Carnegie Hall, "Practice, practice, practice!"

Need some inspiration? Look at quilt patterns, parquet floors, tiles, wallpapers. Printed fabrics can help. So can interesting weaves in tweeds and in knit fabrics. One of the most fertile fields of design inspiration is men's ties. Another great field is bed linens. Printed cocktail napkins are a bonanza. And, of course, there's always the wonderful, inexhaustible world of Aran knits.

The field is wide open and only your own hesitation to explore can limit you. So plunge right ahead, my friend; I wish you Happy Stitchery indeed.

Blocking

Cover a flat wooden surface with aluminum foil and then with brown paper on which you'll draw, with an indelible, waterproof marker, an outline of the size you want the completed design area to be. Use a T-square or right-angle to make sure corners are square. Please don't "eyeball" it—the inaccuracy can be disastrous in the end result. Mark the centers of each side of the drawn outline and the centers of each side of your canvas.

Soak the finished canvas briefly in Woolite and cool water according to manufacturer's instructions. Rinse and roll in a heavy towel. *Do not wring.*

Fasten the needlepoint right side up with rustproof pushpins or tacks. Using your outline as a guide, begin tacking at the centers of the sides, ½ inch in from the canvas edges. Continue to divide and subdivide areas between tacks until you have a border of tacks every ½ inch.

Leave your needlepoint on the blocking board to dry for at least forty-eight hours, seventy-two if necessary in humid or wet weather. Make certain your blocked needlepoint is drying away from direct heat, sunlight, or radiators. Keep the board lying flat to avoid any sagging of canvas. Do not remove it from the board until drying is complete.

Index of Stitches